To: Father, John Van Deuren
From: Bob & Diane Lui

MW00564712

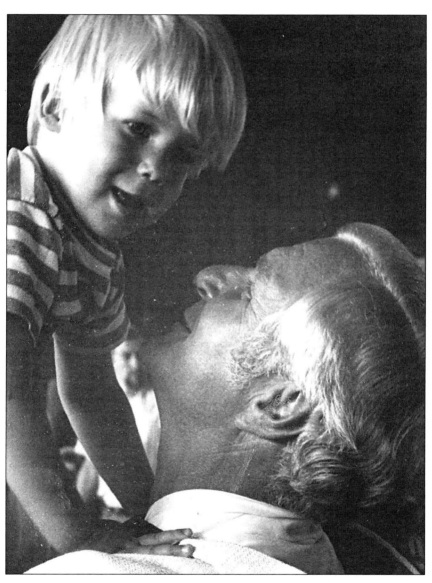

Young friend: Fr. Mauthe with Eric Olson

Once in Love, Always in Love

Fr. Ducs

Fr. Richard Mauthe
& Adi Redzic

ISBN-10: 0-9834384-2-0
ISBN-13: 978-0-9834384-2-7

Authors
Fr. Richard Mauthe and Adi Redzic

Editorial Team & Consultants
Karolyn Efferson, Samantha Haas, Daniel Lestarjette,
Sue Pankratz, Nevena Prebiracevic, Fr. Tom Reynebeau, and Kevin Strack.

Cover Design
Daniel Lestarjette

Cover Photo
Wayne Efferson

Prayer of Saint Francis

Lord, make me an instrument of your peace.
Where there is hatred, let me bring love.
Where there is offense, let me bring pardon.
Where there is discord, let me bring union.
Where there is error, let me bring truth.
Where there is doubt, let me bring faith.
Where there is despair, let me bring hope.
Where there is darkness, let me bring your light.
Where there is sadness, let me bring joy.
O Master, let me not seek as much
to be consoled as to console,
to be understood as to understand,
to be loved as to love,
for it is in giving that one receives,
it is in self-forgetting that one finds,
it is in pardoning that one is pardoned,
it is in dying that one is raised to eternal life.

Amen.

Table of Contents

FOREWORD

Back in 1989, Stephen Covey wrote *Seven Habits of Highly Effective People*, a book purchased by over fifteen million people. Some consider this a business management book. In reality, it is a book about life and has many spiritual overtones.

Father Richard R. Mauthe was an effective priest, a friend to so many, and a character of the first order, blessed with many charisms. He incarnated the principles in Covey's book: he was both efficient and effective in his ministry. As I reflect on Fr. Mauthe's life and ministry I witness a person who responded to Jesus's mission: "I have come that they may have life, life to the full" (John 10:10). Fr. Mauthe lived life to the full. Here are the seven habits, and my take on how they exemplify Fr. Mauthe's life.

"Be proactive." In other words, make things happen. Life can be reactive, simply responding to what comes one's way. For self-starters and those with initiative, life is one of rich creativity. Fr. Mauthe was a leader who had a vision of his priesthood, and what God called him to be and do. A primary example of being proactive was the building of the Ecumenical Center at University of Wisconsin-Green Bay.

"Begin with the end in mind." St. Ignatius of Loyola asserted, "We came from God, we belong to God, we are going home to God." The grand narrative of our creation, redemption, and sanctification was embedded in Fr. Mauthe's mind and heart. While fully engaged in the culture and history of our times, he also had an eschatological sense—our true country is with the Lord. His preaching and teaching reflected this truth.

"Put first things first." What really matters in life? What are our priorities? In a culture that honors the four P's—pleasure, power, possessions, prestige—one can be easily sidetracked down dead-end streets. Not Fr. Mauthe. It was relationships—with God, with others, with oneself, with creation—that held central significance in his life and work. He got it right.

"Think win-win." Competition is a way of life for many of us. It's us against them, it's winners and losers. But then there is a lifestyle of collaboration, a working together for the common good. Fr. Mauthe had a deep social sense and an appreciation for the significance of community. His affable personality and gracious hospitality made people seek his company. His life was about service.

"Seek first to understand, then be understood." This is the land of empathic listening. Fr. Mauthe loved language and was gifted with eloquence. Some may have considered him more talker than listener, but when he was in his pastoral mode, he listened with great attention and compassion. He understood the human condition; he understood and listened to the joys and sorrows of others. He had good ears.

"Synergize." Synergizers are individuals who create momentum by inviting people to come together and share. This was one of Fr. Mauthe's chief charisms: gathering diverse groups of people to come and share. He did what Pope Francis asks us to do: encounter and accompany. Fr. Mauthe had a presence that attracted people and often led to lifelong friendships. He was first cousin to the Energizer Bunny.

"Sharpen the Saw." One habit of effective (and holy) people is balance: time for worship and work, leisure and love. Fr. Mauthe found contemplative time at this cottage in Door County; he worked his tail off at the university; he experienced leisure in Wisconsin summers and quite evenings; his love found a home in friendships and community.

Fr. Richard R. Mauthe was an effective disciple, a faithful friend, and a committed priest. The formation of good habits brought consistency and creativity to his life. He served well. He enjoyed life. He is truly missed.

Bishop Robert F. Morneau
Auxiliary Bishop Emeritus of Green Bay
September 2017

THE IDEA FOR THIS BOOK

I met Fr. Mauthe in 2009, when I joined the then-Ecumenical Center as Director of Development, Marketing, and Programs. Although, at that point, he had been retired from the Center for nearly two decades, Father's spirit still permeated the establishment. Committed to honoring the past, we seized on this spirit and energy for the benefit of the Center's future. In the years that followed, guided by the founder's spirit, we transformed the struggling operation into a thriving hub of student development, spiritual exploration, and service. We also honored Father's legacy by naming the Center after him. The change matched the times we lived in, and it ushered a new day for the more than fifty-year-old organization. It also did something else: it epitomized what one person's vision, determination, diligence, and tenacity can do in the long run. As is often the case in the stories like this one, what started as a part-time gig grew into a one-of-a-kind venture, impacting the lives of thousands, and drawing the fuel from the well of inspiration and personal experiences of the founder.

During my time at the Center, one of my jobs was to tell its story. Promoting activities is one thing, but capturing the essence of a place—and the identity of a living founder—is an entirely different matter. To do it, I needed to get deep into the trenches, getting to know Fr. Mauthe in a meaningful way. *What were his motivations? What were his unique skills? What drove him to dedicate his life to building an interfaith center on a public university, and how did he succeed against many odds?* Perhaps it was my own upbringing in the former Yugoslavia, where different religions and ethnicities fought wars against each other, or a childhood marked by rejection that allowed me to create the emotional connection and find the right words to encapsulated the Center's—and Mauthe's—most authentic narrative. Somehow, the deed was done, and in the process we were all positively affected. Then, I was off to graduate school in Chicago and to run other ventures, locally and nationally. Likewise, the bond between Father and me, and the Center and me, was also formed, but like with most things in life, no one suspected the mysterious paths that would bring us back together.

That is, until May 2016, when I found myself in the area and decided to stop by the Center for the Tuesdays with Mauthe program where Father was being honored. It was a surprise visit and a wonderful reunion. It was also a kismet (an act of God's grace, if you will), because as I began to listen to all those who shared their stories about Father, including some high-powered individuals who were moved to tears as they recalled their interactions with this man, it struck me: *What happens when he dies? Will his unique story—an unbreakable chain of ifs, a daring vision, and a considerable amount of grit—be remembered in a way that is not only historical or biographical, but also very personal?*

Written stories have the ability to capture people's imagination and—a few good ones—the power to move a human heart, bolting the reader with a dose of inspiration and urgency to act. My hope with this project is that Fr. Mauthe's story can do both for some other dreamers, in this community and beyond, inspiring them to dare greatly in a pursuit of a just world, and urging them to fall in love with something greater than themselves—the way Father did. Because once they are in love with the right kind of a thing, they will always remain there and we will all be better for it.

Pa, as Fr. Mauthe was endearingly known by thousands, loved the idea of the book and was a generous partner in putting it together. Most of it is written in the first person, in his voice, and for a reason: we hoped to avoid a traditional biographical narrative in exchange for a unique, personal, even intimate portrayal of his life. I, for one, believed that such a narrative would have a far greater impact on a reader, both in getting to know the protagonist and also in connecting with the deeper wisdom which drove his life. As for Mauthe, he had hoped that his book would live on after he was gone, inspiring and helping as he had done his entire life.

Consequently, we spent a lot of time together, in person and on the phone, talking about his varied and rich experiences. Likewise, he also spoke a lot about the state of affairs in the world today, both temporal and spiritual, injecting philosophical notions on a regular basis. His insights were full of inspiration and wisdom, an occasional warning here and there, and a lot of his unmistakable, if often mischievous, sense of humor. In true fashion, Mauthe also did not want to be the lone voice in this book and asked that some of his friends, who are able, contribute a word or two about their encounters with him. He'd sadly remind me, with a sense of gratitude and apprehension in his voice, even nostalgia, that many from the old days have now passed away. Yet, in line with his generally optimistic persona, he also remained hopeful that those still living would contribute. And they have; the book is filled with insights from people far and wide who have been touched by Mauthe in one way or another. These individuals also represent only the tip of the proverbial iceberg of those who could have written, a leading dozen in a chorus of those who have loved Mauthe and whom he loved back.

As for me, I have been deeply humbled by his trust: he was vulnerable and profoundly open with me. This openness made this project extraordinary as it allowed me to follow in the footsteps of his life's journey to uncover gems of history, entice inspiration of which Mauthe was full, and get to the core of who this person was. But it also made it very challenging: *How do you capture a larger-than-life human being through written word, in his own voice, and do so authentically while also pursuing the utmost accuracy and honoring the discretion afforded by such a relationship?*

Well, you'd ask him. That is what gave me the confidence at the inception of this project and over the months that followed. I'd call him or stop by to read a chapter or two, and then ask for his feedback. Often, he'd interrupt to inject an additional story, remind me of the one not yet written, or—on a few especially meaningful occasions—tell me that he was virtually listening to himself. In those moments, I felt quite victorious, and those agonizing weeks of trying to write a paragraph or two seemed quite inconsequential, because his approval meant we were on the right track. He was my "barometer." I also secretly thought that by working on this book together, he would find the motivation to keep going, even as his health deteriorated greatly and even as he, quite often, wished for his Creator to take him home.

Then, January 12, 2017 came, and as I watched this giant's life come to a close, I found myself wondering, *How the hell am I going to finish this project without Mauthe's guidance or his inspiration?* While we had the majority of it done, there remained a question of quality that indeed only he could have accurately judged.

Fr. Dick Mauthe was a complex individual, deeply intellectual and profoundly spiritual, but a human being nevertheless. He carried his cross openly: his wound of abandonment from birth, his unquenchable thirst for love, his craving for justice, and his uncanny ability to envision what never was and go for it, however inadequately or impatiently. He stood at the forefront of thousands of relationships, giving generously of himself, often demanding more than many could give back, but always pushing the envelope in all he did. As a priest, he was the son of the Church whom he loved like any child loves their parent, yet he often criticized the archaic ways in which his beloved Mother struggled to live up to the needs of the world of today. To him, it was rarely about the systems or the structures and always about the person before him, and he never hesitated to delve deeper into a relationship with that person—and thousands of others—for whom he thought he could be of service; yet, he remained uncommitted to anything but his mysterious dance with God and with life.

At Pa's funeral, Fr. Brice spoke about a lion of a man, who always stood tall even in the face of opposition, soothing the world's injustices, and bringing peace to discord and love to the abandoned, never sitting still while there was unfinished business. Indeed, the business of loving one another and finding ways to serve the world is an ongoing affair. Mauthe knew this well, even as he sacrificed some of his greatest desires in exchange for making this world only a little better. He wasn't perfect, of course, and left some rumble in his path; then again, which change-maker has not ruffled some feathers? Fascinatingly, as much as he was a towering figure in so many people's lives, for some of us who had the privilege of knowing him well, he was indeed a lion, but also a person: flawed, struggling, confused, and a deeply enthralling individual, finding his way in the world.

Spending time with Pa was a gift, as was his vulnerability in the very twilight of his illustrious, if sometimes rough and troubling, life. This book is only a drop in the sea of stories, emotions, and wisdom Father held within, and I am keenly aware of the inherent weaknesses of a manuscript such is this one. Yet, I am grateful for the opportunity to have known someone like him, and to have attempted to help scribe what we called "his final sermon."

   In that spirit, I hope that these words have done justice to Father's story, to some of those who have surrounded him over the years, and to the broader narrative of the Mauthe Center and the interfaith dialogue, and that the words contained herein will move you, if only a little, to believe that when it is all said and done, love is still and always the best choice.

Adi Redzic
June 28, 2017
(Father Mauthe's Birthday)

INTRODUCTION

L ife is a marvelous constellation of "ifs," a wondrous romance of faith and reason, a dance of destiny and choice, which, like an unforgettable opera, moves us through the story of our life with grace and beauty, unfailingly challenging us to reach for the deepest within us and to make this world worthy of God having created it. One road always leads to another, each rendering a life full of experiences: sometimes painful, and at other times soothing, but always enriching and educational. The Apostle Paul wrote to the Corinthians about faith and hope, and the greatest of them all: love. Our life is meant for many things, but among these, in my estimation, love still remains the most important one.

My life, too, has been a beautiful constellation of "ifs." When Onnie and Ray Mauthe gave me a home on that early spring day in 1930, they changed the course of my life forever. When a second call to serve God came during a retreat at Marquette University, some twenty years later, another "if" transcended the ordinary to put me on the path of service to Him, and to my fellow kin. And, when Bishop Bona at first, and then later Bishop Wycislo, tasked me with building a Newman Center (later Ecumenical Center, and now the Richard Mauthe Center for Faith, Spirituality, and Social

Justice) at the University of Wisconsin-Green Bay, little did I know that a journey of a priest earmarked for parish work would grow into a lifelong effort to break the barriers, bringing seemingly disparate groups together, and seeking ways to care for our brothers and sisters from all walks of life—wounded and blessed alike.

Late at night, as I lay bare in my bed gratefully surrendering to my Creator yet another day on this Earth, and as the moon casts its glow over the extraordinary world of ours and as all God's creation rests, I have often wondered about the "ifs" in my life. What would have become of me had I not been adopted? What if my parents were less than wonderful, and what if my odyssey had taken me into law, or finance, or medicine, or a life without a brother or a sister, instead of spirituality? What if some of my early experiences weren't those of rejection, or of bigotry? Would I have still found the strength, or the inspiration, or the will to seek interfaith dialogue among university students in the Northeast Wisconsin community? What if I had fallen in love with only one person instead of many? What if I had not met so many tremendous and beautiful people during my pilgrimage who have colored my life in the most striking and impactful ways, and made my living and my work worthwhile and, indeed, possible? Would I have become the same person, fulfilled and grateful, as I am today?

As I enter the eighty-eighth year of my life, I have a keen vantage point from which to observe and reflect upon all that has come before me: good, bad, and otherwise; the greatest of my deeds and the failures alike. I also have the blessing of a good memory to recall the wonderment that my life has been. It's been a wonderful life. Sure, rejection and struggle have been frequent visitors; so have loneliness and self-doubt at times, but my Creator has blessed me with so much love, the kind that is both unconditional and unending, to which I owe my undying gratitude, and which has made it all worthwhile.

About a year ago, I had a close encounter with death. While preparing for my annual Super Bowl party and waiting for some company to come over, I fell and lost consciousness. What followed was the most horrific of hallucinations: I was being thrown from one side of the Pit to the other, while the eternal flame burned beneath me. I begged to die. I was ready to die. But then, I woke up in a rehab community, surrounded by much love, and with a deep feeling that God was not yet done with me. As if He'd said, "You have one more task before you, one more dance left." Perhaps this task is to tend to my fellow retirees at the retirement community or to pen this book, but whatever it is, I am grateful for another chance to see, to hear, to create, to feel, and to love. God unsettled my soul to remind me that I am not yet finished, and that I cannot be complacent in sharing His love, in making sure that all of His children feel it.

Most of life is boring except for the living part. My life has been interesting. It has also been instructive. But, unlike what some of you may think, I actually never thought it would be worthy of a book. Until a young man, a dear friend of mine who once helped rejuvenate the Mauthe Center on the UWGB campus and is the co-creator on this project, approached me with the idea of writing a book, suggesting that there is still music left in me—music, jokes, and perhaps even some kernels of wisdom that I could impart through the written word. And so, I took up the challenge of going down the memory lane—a long memory lane—in order to compose my life's sermon. It is not a manifesto, because I still remain a student on a quest for truth and evidence, but it is, perhaps, a kind-of memoir, chronicling the various experiences that have made my life what it is and that have taught me one of the most profound lessons: *once we are in love, we are always in love.*

If we are fortunate, many times in our lives we'll be placed in positions to say, "I do," to confess our love for someone or something, and to give our commitment. When we say "I do" at the altar, or in the confines of a private space, or even as we ask for God's grace and love and forgiveness, we may do so with little awareness of the consequence, but the consequence is that we cannot come into love and fall out of it. God does not do that; God does not love us today, then not love us tomorrow. His love is unconditional. So, too, when we confess our love, we feel what we feel, and for a reason; we are ready to fight, to argue, to bargain, and sometimes even grieve if the love isn't truly returned, but we never really stop loving. If you love once, you will always love. The shapes will change, but the essence will remain. I have experienced this throughout my life.

And, so, I hope the words in this book have the power to move you, to make you think, to inform you. I also hope they can shed a bright light on the experiences of a man, of a son and a brother, of a priest, of a friend, of a dreamer who aspired to take God's love and share it with others, regardless of their backgrounds, their color, their creed, their nationality, their wealth, their sexuality, their … anything. I am by no means perfect. But, I have loved deeply, unequivocally, and genuinely, because that is what our Creator has done. That is what we are meant to do. When we love, we bring light where there is darkness, and we find ourselves in the same ranks with our Creator: divine, peaceful, and purposeful.

As we traverse through the waters of my life's journey in the pages that follow, and reflect upon various events, people, and lessons, I hope we can, together, derive new insights in order to capture the essence of what may make this world a little better, a little kinder, more beautiful and, certainly, a lot more loving. I never really wanted to be more than a peaceful parish priest, but when we are called to serve, and to love, it is our duty to answer that call; when we feel moved by something so deeply within us, however scary or imperfect it may appear, as Jesus taught us, we must move forward with it. We must believe.

It is this belief that gives us the strength and the courage to transcend the ordinary, overcome obstacles, and recognize our purpose in life's experience—however happy or sad it may have been. It is this purpose that gives us meaning and strength to love fiercely, now and always.

Fr. Dick Mauthe
July 2016

THE EARLY YEARS

I t was a sunny day on March 30, 1930 when Onnie and Ray Mauthe took their adopted baby boy home. The baby, now almost a year old, was left by a fifteen-year-old mother at a Catholic orphanage run by the Sisters of Misericord from Montreal, Canada for unwed mothers in Green Bay, Wisconsin. After five years of trying to become parents, that spring, their prayers were answered through adoption. The long-awaited dream was realized, and this young, religiously diverse couple fell in love with their new baby. They were parents now, and not even the looming Great Depression could interfere with their joy. They named him Richard.

Of course, this baby was me, and Onnie and Ray Mauthe were two human beings sent by God in a moment of profound grace to shine a bright light on me and my life. They gave me a home filled with love and support, and taught me a great many lessons about living. Through their unconditional love, kindness, generosity, and deep wisdom, they showed me, as my mother liked to say, that it matters not how we are born, only how we grow up.

My mother, Leona (Onnie) Sawall Mauthe was a skinny, fashionable woman with dark, curly hair, and a big, beautiful smile. She was pretty, gregarious, and kind, and she maintained a deep zest for learning throughout her life.

As a librarian at the Kimberly Public Library, Onnie understood the power of books and of education, and early on, she began to instill the love of learning and books in me. She also imbued me with the deep love of God and taught me about His power and presence in my life, as well as His love for me. To her, reason and faith waltzed together; the more she learned, the more convinced of God's presence she was.

Leona and Raymond Mauthe

My father, Ray, was a gentleman. Simple and quiet, he was a deeply compassionate and kind man who maintained a steadfast commitment to caring for his family throughout his life. He worked as a chemist at the Kimberly-Clark paper mill, making about $19 a week during the Depression. One of my favorite memories from childhood was observing my father's initials above the garage door at our family home: it read, RAM (for Ray Albert Mauthe), and I often wondered if it was an initial or an invitation!

As I look back, it seems to me that some people just know how to do the whole parenting thing. Ray and Onnie certainly did. Perhaps it was their deep desire for a child, or their extraordinary spirit and wisdom, but they simply got it. It was never complicated with them; it was deep and sincere, and the experience of it all—and the wisdom that came from it—lasted a lifetime.

My mom was very insistent on some simple truths. I remember, as a small child of four, during one hot summer afternoon, sitting alone under the tree outside the kitchen window when my friend Tommy came by and asked if I wanted an ice cream. Of course I did! So we went to Mr. Kokke's neighborhood store, and while the owner wasn't looking, my friend stole two ice creams: one for him and one for me. He gave me one, and we quickly ran. I knew we had done something wrong, but in those days of scarcity when parents taught us that the sound of the ice cream truck actually meant the truck was out of ice cream—because they couldn't afford to buy us some and didn't want us to ask—a chance to snatch one was too big a temptation.

At home, my mother came out the back door and, after seeing me with the ice cream, she asked about it, surpised:

"Who gave you a nickel for it?"

I told her it was Tommy who bought the ice creams for us. This answer seemed to satisfy her and she went about her business. However, a few hours later, she took me along to the store to get some lunch meat and also, unbeknownst to me, help me face up to my own lie.

As I encountered Mr. Kokke at the store, I excitedly said, "Hello, Mr. Kokke. How are you today?" As if surprised by my greeting, my mother asked me, "Why are you greeting Mr. Kokke as if you hadn't seen him today? Didn't you see him only a couple of hours ago when you and Tommy bought the ice cream bars?" I don't know whether she knew from the outset that those ice cream bars weren't purchased, or whether my greeting tipped her off, but I knew in that moment that my lie had been discovered. Mr. Kokke's response didn't help either. As if they were colluding, Mr. Kokke calmly said, "Those kids weren't here earlier; they got no ice cream bar from me today."

Terrified, I screamed out: "Tommy made me do it!"

She looked me straight in the eye and told the owner, "Whenever you see him at the store, treat him as a thief." Then she sternly told me to never lie or steal again, regardless of the circumstances. Needless to say, I have never stolen or lied since.

My parents had some real values about truth, honesty, and how we treat one another, but deep truths were often taught over simple matters, and that is how it all began.

I learned early on about tolerance and care for others, too. When Onnie's mother, Emma Berharndt Sawall, had a stroke, and she could not speak, or walk, or remember, my mother—who was one of nine children—moved her in with our family. This was during the Depression. To make room for Grandma, I was moved out of my room to the attic. We had a bungalow with a small, slanted roof, but it was not heated, so when winter came they moved my bed down next to the furnace in the basement. There, between two big round pipes that sent the heat up to the house, is where my bed was placed; and all night long I could hear the agar turn, grinding the coal into the fire pit. There were no thermostats in those days, but the amount of fire we had was determined by a chain that was on the little lift door in front of the stove, and as you lifted it, the heat intensified. To control the heat, you simply turned the thing more open or more closed. That's where I remember growing up, in the basement. I don't remember protesting as some children of today might; I was happy to have my sanctuary. That's where I made my imaginary grocery store and my drug store. As my friends came to play, we'd pretend to go to the grocery store: some would want Rice Krispies and some a free ticket to the movies. We lived in a small world that made sense.

As far as I can remember, one of my favorite pastimes was pretending to be a priest. I would arrange my room in such a way as if I were serving mass: a small table in my room was my altar, the dish on it the holy chalice, and a sheet or a bathrobe, my priestly garb. Interestingly, it was not a solitude of prayer in which I had found the allure of priesthood, even as a young child, but rather the opportunity to gather in community, as we do when we come together in sadness and joy, when we break bread and celebrate Eucharist. There's nothing more powerful or more connecting to the divine than when we face one another, and find God through each other.

I wonder if children these days play in a similar fashion?

Sometimes I wonder if this simpler world we lived in was also a more peaceful one. As I look around, especially at the youth of today, as much as we have as a society advanced in certain areas, I fear that the distractions they face pose a limitation on their journey to God, to freedom, and to love. Then again, it is all relative. I just hope they will continue to have opportunities to be children, to feel loved, and to be free to be playful. I'll never forget those days of playing with my friends. Life seemed so promising, and indeed it was.

Ray and Onnie Mauthe on their wedding day

My grandma was a simple, humble woman and German Lutheran through and through. Even in her illness and disability, the dedication to her faith was unwavering. Almost every Thursday, a local pastor (I think his last name was Wickman) would come in and bring Grandma the Communion. As she sat quietly in a rocker chair in our dining room, shawl over her shoulders and with a humble, pensive look, the Pastor would thunder in speech at her—as if she were a Cathedral. Quoting St. Paul's letter, he would proclaim, "He has brought us together! Er hat uns zusammengebracht!"

As he stood there from week to week, a towering person of authority, speaking in German and pounding at the dining room table at this one person—small in stature but large in spirit—with a zest and conviction, I found myself understanding the power of the language and the rhetoric. His few

sentences had a profound impact on my grandmother; like a drug, she was mesmerized with his presence, with his words, and his energy: he helped elevate her from a state of disability to a state of hopefulness. This gift of words, and of God's work, evoked emotion which gave meaning to my grandma, it strengthened her, and from week to week, kept her significantly weakened mind engaged and faithful. To my young mind, this was awesome and impactful.

Leona (Sawall) Mauthe with her mother, Emma Sawall

That wasn't the only impression my young self derived from this adventure. His words, and the entire experience, were also telling me that something was uniting that had previously been separated. Confused, one day, I finally asked my mom:

"What was it that grandma was uniting?"

She passionately uttered, "It wasn't Grandma, my child, it was God who was uniting the Christians." As a fairly small child, I didn't fully understand the implication or the depth of this sentiment, but these words of unity—diametrically opposed to the practice of divisiveness—have stuck with me my entire life.

Even though my Grandma Emma was a quiet and unassuming woman, as I contemplate my experiences with her, my memories of her seem quite dramatic. Even her death came unexpectedly during our supper one evening, when she suffered a stroke at the dinner table and passed away. My dad jumped straight up to help her, but it was too late. She was gone. I was about ten years old when she died, leaving me with a very early impression of how fleeting and short our lives are. Life can, and often does, end when we least expect it. And even when someone had been sick for a while, we are still left unsettled when they're finally gone. Having our grandma live with us was a gift that not many are afforded these days, and the lessons from her life endure. Truly, my parents' decision to care for her was also an important lesson in compassion and selfless love.

My Grandpa Edward Sawall, who died five years prior, was a demanding man as much as my Grandma Emma was a tender loving woman. As I was much younger when he died, I do not have many memories of him. However, I do remember one time (I must have been four or five), a rooster from my grandfather's farm took off and landed on my head. Grandpa took his straw hat off, flung it at its side, and chased the rooster off my head. To a child, this was an adventure like no other; I remember giggling, carefree and joyful, like only a child can be.

I also remember my grandpa speaking to me in German. He loved to quote the famous German proverb, "Was gut genug für den König ist, ist gut genug für dich." What's good enough for the king is good enough for you. As with Pastor Wickman's words about unity, my grasp of the wisdom behind this saying in those days was limited, but what stuck with me was the letter and the meaning of equality. If what's good enough for a king, and perhaps vice versa, it must mean, ultimately, we all deserve the same kind of things regardless of outward differences. By the same token, ironically, it was early in life that I also learned the differences between Lutheran and Catholic, not theologically but viscerally. In those days the differences were quite stark. Even though I was taught that there was no difference between people following each faith—they were both deserving of the same things—I also learned early on that there was divisiveness, and my parents' own experiences paved the way for this important awareness.

Onnie and Ray were the envy of the community, and an example of an extraordinary couple. They were a team, in the best sense of that word, always finding ways to collaborate, challenge, and support each other, and never failing to love deeply and passionately. Many years later, in the twilight of my father's life, he'd ask me to shave his face, the way my mother used to do. It was this small gesture, the smoothness of his face, that would remind him of her touch and their life together, which by that point, he had missed for a very long time.

Onnie and Ray knew the lessons of love, and understood that once we are in love, we are always in love. One may argue that they fell in love through mutual affinity and attraction, but that they learned the true meaning of love through much practice and a lot of effort. Their backgrounds were stark for that time: my mother came from a strict, deeply German Lutheran background; my father was a Catholic. Fortunately, things have changed for the better since then, but in those days a love, a union, between Onnie and Ray was scandalous. Thankfully, their love prevailed over the very real opposition. Collectively, there was opposition in the theoretical sense, derived from the theological differences, which fueled the persistent, practical opposition: shaming, frowning-upon, and exclusions. I was only a baby when some of my own kin suggested to my parents they better keep me, their Catholic child, and their Catholic selves, at a distance for we did not worship their God; I was a "Papist." *What had a baby done to them?* I was clearly enough for God to place me on this Earth, yet I was less than enough for other humans, who used God's name to justify their bigotry.

This is not a nod to the bigotry then present in the Protestant community—my fellow Catholics weren't much better either. In many ways they rejected the Protestants with the same fervor. And there certainly was little or no mention of our Jewish, Muslim, Buddhist, or any other kind of brethren in faith. The lines of divisiveness were drawn clearly, and strictly enforced. For a boy barely old enough to dress himself, such explicit rejections were both confusing and deeply impressionable.

Thankfully, my parents found a way to bring me up with malice toward no one, including those who rejected us, and only a desire to rest in God and his love for us. My mother liked to say, "Be competitive as all beings, but never defeat anybody just to put them down." I have tried to heed her advice throughout my life, if sometimes imperfectly. It also took me a while to see the fine distinction in her assertion. When we pursue things we deem important, the things we are called to do, and our focus isn't to put others down— to beat them—then, should it happen that we do win, the victory will be humble, allowing others their dignity, and perhaps they will come along on a journey with us, coexisting peacefully. When we focus on beating others—like much of the politicians do today, for example—the best possible outcome is a Pyrrhic victory, benefiting no one. In other words, focusing on our purpose may leave some people behind, but that will be a by-product of a larger goal. We are not after them just to defeat them because they're somehow—due to some narrow-minded, thoughtless, and selfish thinking—lesser than us. On the other hand, when we compete to beat others—which, I have observed many do—competing is no longer the objective; beating the other guy is. Onnie and Ray taught me that there's enough space for all of us in God's house, and certainly enough blessings and enough love to go around without having to take even a drop of it away from anyone else.

As I look back at this period of my life, I understand how my parents have set me on a path of inviting and welcoming all God's children into the fold. And, to this day, I remain baffled at the idea that some people are still shunned by the Church; the place where we are meant to come together in peace, respect, and mutual understanding. These early experiences lit the way for me to see that if we embrace God and love God, and also grasp His unending and unconditional love for us, we must expect and demand of ourselves to love all of God's creation, too. *How could we not? How can we ask to be loved, pursue love, take the love, yet fear that in giving love something may be taken from us?*

Many years ago, I was asked by a young student, "What if we are not loved back? Or worse, what if they don't live as they should, according to the word of God or our opinion?" The answer to that quandary is simple: so what? We are not in the business of loving others or loving a cause just because we expect it to love us back; that's a transaction, not a genuine expression of love. If we love something or someone, we love because that is what we feel, not because of a response, or a reward, we may receive. We love or we don't love, but it is our love to give, not our love to exchange when convenient or for a prize. Furthermore, if we don't love, does that mean we need to hate and reject? I think not. And my reading of the Holy Scripture supports this: Jesus of Nazareth brought all into his fold and strictly forbade judgment. Yet, I see so many judge and condemn others in His name, and it pains me. Sometimes I see people pretend not to judge, but they still do, making themselves hypocritical on top of being judgmental. And that pains me even more. We were not put on this Earth to hate. We will not love all, but to close the door to God is to betray the very divine essence that resides in each one of us. So, I told that student—and thousands of others before and since—that if they turn anyone from the love of God, or from the holy Church, they may as well turn Jesus from it. In God's house, there is room for all of His creation. So indeed, in retrospect, it is quite obvious why I found my calling as a priest, and a voice for interfaith dialogue, mutual respect, and understanding. Considering my earliest experiences, it only made sense.

It was early on that I also learned about rigidity that comes with thought. As a librarian, my mother had easy access to books, and would read every book that came into the Kimberly Public Library. She was perhaps a bit of a dreamer, too, like myself, seeking to see what is hidden behind the obvious. Letting our emotion, and our inner imagination, take over from time to time, allows us to see what is seemingly not there yet. In fact, she used to have

Mrs. Ray Mauthe, Librarian at the Kimberly public library, was recently elected president of the Wisconsin Fox Valley Librarians association. Mrs. Mauthe was selected for the post at a conference at Waupun. (Post-Crescent Photo)

this table, way back then in the 1930s, that was only eighteen inches tall and pads to kneel or sit on the floor, so the children at the library (and we at home, too) could sit and read big books, but do so imaginatively. She'd have the children look through the pages of the books without trying to read them, as most of us at that age couldn't really read well, and then ask everyone to formulate stories of what they were seeing. They'd tell narratives created entirely in their own minds, expressing their remarkable and often goofy imaginations, and it was wild! A brilliant way to teach and foster imagination.

On the other hand, my father, would often use experiences like these to provoke intriguing and inspirational questions. He was a practical man, a chemist, and while he obviously understood the power of imagination, he was also concerned about integrating it all with the reality. I remember distinctly one dinner conversation when he paused and then pointedly asked if education was the enemy of imagination. My life, since I can remember, has been filled with inspirational jabs like this one, but this particular question has remained with me ever since. The answer, I think, is yes and no. Yes, to the extent that life without imagination would be only half a life. Most of the things any of us have done have started as dancing fantasies, and then moved to some form of reality. And no, because it is through education that we gain insights and the knowledge that, if properly and analytically embraced, allows the imaginative expansion without limits.

Ultimately, life seems to be a matter of fulfilling what seem to be clichés of what civilization has woven, while allowing new light to seep in, propelling us to new vistas of realization and awareness. Thus, it is the question of finding the balance, an equilibrium of what we have inherited through the ages, and the experiences we often self-choose, using both to color the tapestry on the wall of life.

Then again, there are also those transformative experiences in life that are neither inherited nor self-chosen; they just appear. Like getting a sibling.

When I was five years old, as Onnie and Ray attempted to adopt a baby girl, they learned that they were pregnant. In the midst of the Depression, three children was not an option, so they unfortunately had to let go of the adoption process. A few months later, my brother Ed was born on Valentine's Day, 1935. With him, something tremendous had happened: for the first time in my life, I had a family. Our little home, the first house off Main Street in Kimberly, Wisconsin, gained a new flavor, and became a kind of sanctuary. It was exciting, though one may argue that the enthrallment of this experience dimmed ever so slightly after I learned that this child was not a visitor, and was here to stay as a permanent part of the house!

Joking aside, I, of course, did not know something was missing from my life until Ed's arrival. His birth completed our home. With Ed's arrival, I also learned companionship, friendship, and how to share. The toys weren't all mine anymore. Although the difference of five-plus years between us was substantial and probably caused us to not always be close with each other, in all truth, the fundamental connection between us has always been there.

Richard and Ed Mauthe

Blood looks thin next to our relationship. I can only begin to imagine how different, and empty, my life would have been without Ed.

Our parents never separated us in their treatment, and they used a variety of methods to instill within us a solid moral compass. They wanted to teach deep truths while preparing us both for the real experiences of life. They wanted us to be well-rounded, caring, and hardworking men. My mother, in particular, was an outstanding woman, always looking for new and often profound methods to teach us about imagination, truth, and life as a whole. At the same time, she'd also get practical and teach us things such as how to iron a white shirt, knead bread, and even make a pie crust without touching it too much. (If you want to keep it tender, leave it alone!)

They also taught us hard work by example. In addition to both of them having day jobs, Ray and Onnie held side jobs as correspondents for *The Post Crescent* in Appleton, reporting on events in Kimberly: whether it was a basketball game, a village board meeting, or even an event at the church. They'd come home and sit down; my father would dictate, and my mother would write longhand and then type up the news on the typewriter. The next morning, it was my turn to contribute. My father would get up at five o'clock, and would then get me up. In the winter, I'd put on my corduroy winter suit: bottom part first, then boots, and then the coat. Then, I would walk six blocks to bring the news to *The Post Crescent* editor Greg, who lived in Kimberly, so that he would then get on the bus and take the typed-up news with him to the office at 7:30 a.m.

One weekday morning, in December, I was walking down Main Street to Washington, to give the news to Greg, when I looked through the window of the house where my friend and classmate Mike lived, only to see his mother and father decorating a Christmas tree. *What in Santa's world were they doing?!* This was Santa's job and he only did it in the dark, and we weren't allowed to watch. Yet, there I was, witnessing the truth, feeling betrayed and confused, and yet also, for the first time, coming into an inner conflict about whether I should tell my brother Ed what I had seen that morning or whether I should keep my first secret. It was in this innocent experience of learning discipline and hard work that I also discovered the tension between the stories we are told and the truth, which, ultimately, is impossible to hide.

This tension, between the stories we know and the truth we discover, has been at the forefront of much of my work, both inner and what has been done outwardly.

Stories and truth are both parts of the same thing. Every mystery that we have in Christianity has its own background and roots in pageantry and mystique. The simple idea of God becoming a Man in the incarnation is almost too willing a truth to be conceived. Most of us operate out of some sense of gain, which then begs the questions: *What does God have*

Ray Mauthe with Dick

to gain from coming? We are introduced to a quandry, wandering in the fields of experiences in the pursuit of truth. Why would He take on a Body that needs to be fed, a Mind that needs to be nourished, and a Spirit that needs to reside in the limited human form? Why would He do all of that, He who has the eternal wisdom? If He is truly divine, what does He need to know that He doesn't already?

As a spiritual being and a priest, I have come to believe that the simple answer is love. We are so overwhelmingly loved by God, that in reaching out and attempting to bring us to Himself—to understand the very foundational truths about life and love—His hope is that in the moments of intimacy with Him, He will teach us to love one another. Of course, intimacy takes different forms for different people. For example, when you read John of the Cross or Teresa of Avila, the foremost Christian mystics, they talk about intimacy with God using sexual expressions. From their points of view—and I don't know how that came about—they learned something profound. The quest itself was the experience, to say nothing about the reality of the grasp.

This logic, however, necessitates another question: if God has done all this, why don't we then love one another? The world is full of examples of humans falling short from this ideal. It is really a mystery, isn't it? Why we simply can't love one another selflessly? Theologically, one may say, it comes down to free will, but there is more to it. Over the years, I have come to believe that we live out of fear that something will be taken from us, and even if we give something away, it won't be replaced, returned, or reciprocated. This can be money, beliefs, kindness, or even love. This fear drives us to cling to scarcity instead of embracing abundance; judge generosity and advocate for reciprocity; and rarely take the first step to compassion, forgiveness, giving, and understanding. We don't easily give of ourselves, yet—ironically—we are quick to ask it of others, and ask a lot. Or, on the contrary, we may not ask, we simply close off. We reason: "I will keep everything I have to maintain at least my own personal solidarity and the view of life; my own world-vision." As for others, our fear tells us, they're not as important. We replace a vast vision of God's Kingdom on Earth with our pretty little fearful fence.

But then, the inquiry continues: Where does the fear come from?

Ultimately, we want to go back to our lover, who happens to be our Creator. St. Augustine explained this well when he said that our hearts are restless until they rest in Him. And restlessness has lots of fears built into it: about the future, the past, the possibilities, the limitations, and, certainly, about our end. Therefore, the next question in this thought process is: How do we fall in love with God? How do we rest our hearts?

One time, I saw a message on a wallboard in a subway that simply said: *Let God.* And I think the implication was: you tried money, you tried power, you tried control, now let go. We rest our hearts in Him by letting go, by accepting, and by trusting.

How do we do that? Well, who we are and *how we are* is from God. Our job is to continue to seek evidence for the truths we have been taught, as well as to ask questions about the stories we have been told. Ray and Onnie have taught me a great many truths, all of which have washed over in a lot of areas of my life. They worked with me through the theological concepts, and gave me the strength to maintain perspective in the face of other people's truths. Every time I hear a "religious truth" espoused by somebody, I tell myself, "This person believes that as much as I do what I believe. It is not for me to judge if something is true or not. The truth does not need my protection; she knows her own way."

I have accepted the fact that each of us is made unique, each of us thinks uniquely, each of us finds a different way to find relevancy, and each of us ends up with a behavior that matches our intellectual grasp of an issue. Therefore, in order to honor our unique journey and perspective, it is our job to respect the same in others. Of course, this is not always welcome news to everybody who thinks that the world needs to conform to what they believe, but I don't blame them. I try to have compassion for their struggle because—fundamentally—they need to know there is some truth. This knowledge offers a sense of security, and sometimes even esures survival. And given all the "truths" that are out there, as well as all the half-truths, untruths, mistruths, misunderstood truths, or truths that meant something at one time but don't at another, it can get quite confusing. It is also scary not to stick with a truth that is comfortable, even if it is inadequate, judgmental, or exclusionary.

There are a lot of things that I believe that the Apostles never knew. For example, they never knew the immaculate conception or even said the word Assumption. They did not know of the existence of these concepts, and the needs of the time never called for them. This is perhaps why St. Paul reminds us to have reason for the faith that is within us. As our human experiences multiple, by asking questions and wrestling with them, we strengthen our faith. Each of us fortresses our own truth with our own experiences and with what we have read and what we have been taught. We build walls out of what we believe in, which is what creates the opposition—the literal and figurative barriers—between our respective truths. But if we embrace openness, and the idea that each of us is predisposed in different ways, and that each of us has the right to express our own truths as long as it does not do violence to someone else, then we begin to break down the walls. And if we come as close to whispering as we can, and do so through a very thin tissue paper, so-to-speak, we will find more togetherness, common ground, and closeness to God than if we engaged in shouting matches over our enormous fences. Truth and error aren't that far apart, and as my life has shown time and again, God works in mysterious ways. With openness, we come closer to Him and to one another.

As I contemplate my childhood, walking back and forth down memory lane, and reflect on those earliest experiences and the wonderful people who shaped them, and shaped me, and frame some of the knowledge—wisdom, if you will—that I have acquired over the years, I am left in awe over life's beauty and God's magnificence. Like a well-fitting shoe, it all fits together perfectly well and, to my utter delight, it all makes sense.

Life is a wonderful romance with each person as our dance partner, and we make it together by leading each other home. Although it is inevitable, I never want my dance card to be filled up for there's always one more dance left. I am grateful to my parents, Ray and Onnie, who were my first dance partners, and who taught me, since my earliest days, to break barriers and crush my own walls to let in the light. Doing so allowed me to have more diverse dance partners than I could have ever imagined, thus making my life richer and even more worthy of God's grace. Their lessons have depth in me, too, and have placed me on a quest for evidence for the truth I hold, or even the truth I aspire to, and had it not been for an act of goodness by a loving couple, my life would have been so much different. If someone else had adopted me, if someone else gave bith to me, if I never had a brother ... the matter of "ifs" continues, and I will never truly know how different my life would have been without Ray and Onnie, but I do know that it would not have been nearly as meaningful, or as rich, or as loving.

As these words spill on the paper, and as I sit in my armchair at the Odd Fellow's Home, a marvelous retirement and rehab community in the Green Bay's Astor Park neighborhood, I am astonished that by God's grace I am closing my long life in the very same spot where the orphanage from which I was adopted was established back in the 1920s, and only six blocks from St. Mary's Hospital where I was born on June 28, 1929.

But then, I also chuckle after remembering the words of my good and old, old friend, Bishop Morneau, who told me recently, "Dick, you're the only priest who has two places named after him: 'The Mauthe Center and the Odd Fellow's Home!'" There's some truth to that!

LEGACY OF ADOPTION

Almost every night when I was a child, I'd kneel by my bed next to my mom, and we would pray for my biological mother. This was Onnie's way of teaching me forgiveness and a greater understanding of my life as an orphan. Furthermore, since my earliest days, for Christmas and Easter, my parents would take me to the orphanage I came to see the children who had not been adopted. At the time when being adopted carried a considerable amount of shame, they wanted me to understand that I was indeed adopted, but that my life was in no way lesser than anyone else's; it was just different. They never hid from me that I had been an orphan, because they fully believed there was no shame in it. At some level, they perhaps also wanted to help me see that in the loss of my biological parents, I gained another, hopefully richer life. And they were right. Over the years, each time when I experienced a rejection that, at some level, subconsciously took me back to that earliest experience of being given up by my biological mother—of feeling fundamentally rejected—I witnessed something better happening in my life. It's going back to that constellation of "if's;" I was beyond blessed to have Onnie and Ray raise me, and, indeed, my adoptive parents were my only parents.

At a couple of occasions, first when I was sixteen and then upon my graduation from Marquette, my father wanted to give me my adoption papers. In doing so, he wanted to honor whatever questions may have lingered within me about my adoption or my biological parents. He wanted me to open the papers, perhaps satisfy my curiosity or even seek out my birth mother. But I never wanted to know. In fact, at last attempt to do so, during my graduation party, I threw the papers into the fire-burning stove without ever looking at them.

As we stood there, Mom, Dad, Ed, and I, surrounding the burning documents, I said to them, "I am very satisfied with who you and momma are"—a sentiment that still holds true—"and I don't need to know."

I truly believed that the life Ray and Onnie had given me was so incomparable to anything a biological mother could have done. Of course, I had nothing to compare it with, and we could only speculate. I've done that at times, wondering how different my life would have been had I not been orphaned, but I could never know this with certainty. What I knew was what I had, and those were the facts of my reality. Whatever her reasons may have been, my biological mother did give me away, and even though this reality has burnt my soul throughout my entire life, to seek her seemed insensitive and imprudent to all involved. To me, it would have likely been a very anxiety-inducing journey, even painful. To Ray and Onnie, regardless of what they said at the time, any quest to find my birth mother would have likely felt like a rejection, a slap in the face, if you will—as if I were saying they weren't good enough. I never believed that I could say I loved Ray and Onnie unconditionally and claim them as my one and true parents, and also search for my biological mother. That always seemed duplicitous to me. Finally, I also felt the need to be circumspect even in relation to the woman who had given me away.

My birth mother presumably had a very good reason for giving me up for adoption. Perhaps she had no other choice, or maybe she wanted a better life for me. Whatever the reasons, even if she fundamentally did not want me, my showing up at her door, twenty-plus years later, seemed unwise. I might be unwelcome news. What if she had gotten married, had a new family, and what if none of them knew that I had even existed? Showing up could potentially condemn her, and that was too big a responsibility to carry. Did I have the right to do this? Is it up to me to decide if someone's past ought to be brought up? What if by doing so I destroyed a marriage or harmed people around me in some other way? How do I honor myself while not harming others? At what point do you honor and at what point do you protect? I don't think I had such a clear answer to these questions when I decided to burn the papers, but looking back I have a keen understanding that some people need to know and do certain things, while others don't. In all this, thoughtfulness is really important. Maybe I was afraid that I'd be vengeful towards her. I fundamentally did not (and do not) believe that we need to even out with people; that may be what our ego wants, and it is very tempting, but that is not the point of life. Although they messed up my life in being "normal," it does not mean I get to do the same thing to them: because you did this to me, I can do that to you. I wasn't interested in the eye-for-an-eye game. On the other hand, perhaps I was just too scared of the truth; maybe I did not want to face up to the reality that she did indeed give me up because she did not want me. Maybe I was, not only emotionally or theoretically, but de facto rejected and unloved.

Most people experience a certain degree of abandonment and rejection in life, but being an orphan as a result of your parents willfully giving you away comes with a unique brand of it: your very own kin did not want you, from birth. That is a baggage no orphan ever chose, yet each of us has carried it in our own way, as best as we can. At the same time, the emotional impact of being an orphan is often hard to put into words, and I suspect it is also hard for a person to understand what that is truly like unless they've been there. Walking in one's shoes on something so fundamental, and so fundamentally raw, is very hard—not impossible, but very hard.

Being an orphan comes with a set of consequences that seem to stay with us throughout our lives. From time to time, those consequences—the unique mix of insecurity, pain, emptiness, and longing—

A young sailor

rear their ugly heads, reminding us that we were not wanted from the outset. We are often left feeling a gap, a missing piece in our emotional makeup. It is a dark, often scary, and generally incomprehensible emptiness that is neither logical nor reasonable. Yet, it seems to affect us deeply, particularly in the realm of relationships. You're never quite sure what to make of others, or of your own feelings towards them. Sometimes you give more, sometimes less. Either way, something appears to be off. It's an emotion, not an intellectual reasoning: a feeling of being perpetually misunderstood and inadequate, of having a voice that is not loud enough, and a yearning for the wholeness that often seems close but never close enough to grasp. The void, no matter how big or small at any given time, seems to constantly, if not consistently, appear, leaving us thirsty for more of that which we feel was taken away at the outset: unconditional love. As a result, many of us have found ourselves struggling to remain consistent in our relationships with those who had nothing to do with our "orphan-status." In those self-made relationships, we sometimes feel deeply satisfied, and at other times yearning for a cosmos beyond our own.

I, in particular, am keenly aware that I have at times placed enormous demands on people—demands to love me—out of my own sense of inadequacy and longing. Fortunately for me, my desire for love has been abundantly quenched in ways big and small. It first started with my adoptive parents, my brother, and then it expanded to thousands of others who gave me a part of themselves. This fact alone transforms the orphan's pain into gratitude.

As an orphan, you do not take relationships—or the experience of love—for granted or lightly; therefore, you are bound to desire something so powerful and powerfully meaningful when encountering other people. You want each and every relationship, however impossible this may be, to transcend all others. Only then, it seems, your void and your deep, unexplainable yearning to be loved will be bridged. And often it is ... until it no longer is, and you are strung back, like a marionette, into those earliest, formative moments when those who "should have" loved you, didn't. Sometimes, you feel left out and screwed over, and at other times, this quest for love—deep and god-like—becomes the most wonderful realization: that you, in fact, were fortunate not to have been raised by the people who, ultimately and for whatever reason, gave you away, but were embraced by those who, in fact, wanted you.

Such were Ray and Onnie. I spent a lot of time during my life reminding myself of the blessing they were and working hard to internalize the sense of gratitude to replace the sense of rejection. Perhaps I had the strength to shake off occasional bouts with the feelings of abandonment because Ray and Onnie did a wonderful job of filling in any obvious emotional gaps. And it was all the other people, too, who put

Always in on a joke: quite foxy in the summer of 1945

up with me over the years, because they saw I was searching for the very same thing they were: love.

Looking back, this paradox, of feeling deeply loved and yet not loved enough, placed me in a position in which I had little use for half-baked friendships; you're either a friend or you're not. I also have very little patience for small talk. We either get to know each other, and each other's soul, deeply and fundamentally, and we fall in love with each other, or we don't. A lot of people "network" these days, faking their emotions and replacing real relationships with an appearance of relationship. I guess they can afford it. I couldn't, and never have. Transparency has always been the key. How else do we get to love?

Lastly, it was also God's grace that unequivocally played a big role in all of this, allowing me to fill in the gaps with His inextinguishable love, and express it in the flesh by taking care of those who needed me, by building a table long enough to fit the misfits, regardless of where they came from, and by daring to be vulnerable and honest even when it was hard—even as I felt alone and misunderstood and rejected. It was, ultimately, God's grace which saw me through.

SPEAKING OF GOD...

God works in mysterious ways, never giving us more than we can handle, but always, unequivocally and provocatively, placing us before challenges worthy of our god-like nature. And no matter how much, or how well, we plan for what is to come, it is beyond our human power to know how exactly our lives will unfold, which roads we will travel, and what wisdom—if any—we will acquire on our journey from dust to dust. Yet, every day presents an opportunity to make thousands of decisions, which lead us to new vistas, and which shape our lives in most marvelous of ways. This is especially true when we are faced with a big decision and a profound question: What will I become?

When I was a very young man, even as I played a priest on a regular basis, for some odd reason I still believed I would grow up to be an attorney or a doctor; someone who can concretely, tangibly, and directly contribute to the earthly well-being of my kin. I would draw up some contracts and fight for justice before the courts in our vast judicial system, or perhaps heal the sick and the wounded through the means of the modern medicine. But then, at some point, my childish playfulness met the spiritual pull, allowing me to sense an entirely different calling to serve the world as a Catholic priest. My upbringing, at the

Another big love: tap dancing! As a child, Fr. Mauthe actively performed at various venues across Wisconsin. Later, in college, to support himself, Fr. Mauthe taught tap dance.

intersection of two faith traditions and filled with a persistent religious presence, played a critical role in this desire. But, I think, there was more to it than my upbringing. Perhaps it was a desire for unconditional love, to give and to receive love. Or maybe it was more. There exists an inner call, a yearning, a mystery, which pulls us all to enter into our vocations, and we can rarely give a full account or even understand why it happens. Priests can intellectualize and rationalize why they enter a religious life, but they never really know; they only feel. The depths of our emotions compel us to move forward, guided by the Holy Spirit, and the very divine within us. Just like a bird instinctively sings its song, we too are moved by something far greater than ourselves, and once we embark upon a path the rest simply reveals itself like beautiful yellow begonias. It is not in our hands to determine what happens, we only know that it must happen—one way or another.

And so, very early on, I was willing to give a priestly life a go. My parents, both of them deeply spiritual and faithful, supported me in this endeavor. I was a sophomore in high school when my first dance with God commenced. I joined the Minor Seminary, the St. Lawrence Seminary in Mt. Calvary, Wisconsin. I hoped that this early entry into a religious life would pave my way into becoming a parish priest someday. I also saw no reason to wait. As most teenagers, I was imbued by a zeal for independence, and a deep feeling that my decisions made sense; likewise, I also lacked the depth to understand all the consequences that came with such an enormous step. So, I spent about a year at the seminary, but by the end, it simply became unbearable: I was sad, confused, and homesick, and could no longer stay apart. As a result, I left. I returned home, into the loving fold of my parents and my brother, who did not judge my "failure," and instead rejoiced in having me back. I then went on to complete high school at Kimberly High. But this episode, this quick rendezvous with God, left a bitter taste, reminding me of a passage in the Scriptures where the prophet speaks of being duped, and I too felt this way. I was convinced that priesthood was my path, but why did it not unfold the way I had planned and wanted? It seemed that just as I had it in my grasp, it slipped away into the abyss of no return. What appeared to be there, mine and holy, easy and natural, was suddenly carried away through my own inability to withstand the difficulties that came with answering this call. How could this be? Was I too weak to resist the temptations of the secular life—even if that only meant missing my parents? Was I not made out of the right material for such a profound call? Eventually, I moved the blame from myself to the "destiny" and came to believe that it simply was not meant to be, at least at that moment in time, and that I should be patient and wait for another call from above. While deeply disappointed and perhaps a bit ashamed, as time went on and my wounds healed, I realized that I was simply not yet ready to give up on this "pull" into the spiritual life. I still felt there was more to it, that this business of becoming a priest was long from over.

By the time I graduated high school in 1948, having realized and understood what had happened more fully, and perhaps forgiving myself for failing the first time around, I was ready to try again. This time, I wanted to join the Order of the Capuchin Franciscan Friars. They were open to the idea, but required that I first finish a year-long internship so they could see what I was like, and whether they'd accept me into their fold. It was a type of structured discernment; they wanted me to take a deeper look, to see the world a little bit, and to understand what the outside was like and what I might be giving up. By this point, however, the mystery of vocation had taken over, again. I wanted to enter even more fully into what that was all about, and so eventually I began my journey of becoming one with them. I attended junior college at the Capuchin House of Philosophy in Garrison, New York and lived with them for several years, through the Novitiate, and even professed my Simple Vows. However, just as it appeared that God had responded to my call, smiling at me, and allowing me to pursue the life of service to Him, I was asked to leave before the Solemn Vows could be made. The Provincial did not think I was stable enough to stay on as a priest because, in his view, I was not moldable to his vision of what I was supposed to be like. For one, I failed at complete obedience, which, unsurprisingly, is neither a coincidence nor a surprise, and it is certainly a theme that has followed my priestly career. And two, my ideas seemed to shake up this closely-knit community. I was too independent, they told me. Although I probably knew deep down that they were right, I was nevertheless struck by grief, disappointment, and sorrow.

As a product of my upbringing, the Great Depression, and World War II, I was among the early rebels who had been encouraged and had hoped for the changes eventually brought on by Vatican II. Unbeknownst to me at the time, this eagerness to ask deep questions, promote unity, and find ways to build bridges among my religious brethren and their flock would become a hallmark of my career. Furthermore, it was the intellectual roots, which I grew and nourished from my earliest days, that pushed me back then, have pushed me my whole life, and continue to push me today to ask questions in a quest to deepen my faith. If we cannot challenge and ask and probe in order to pursue the truth, then we are not confident or secure in God or in our faith. It is only natural, in my estimation, to ask questions and to even challenge what once was, and our experience of it all, because only then do we get closer to God. If the divine were so shallow, we would have long ago re-entered the Garden of Eden, or reached Nirvana and Enlightenment, or whatever it may be. But it is not so simplistic. It requires depth and inner work. Thinking that we have all the definite, final answers takes God's grace, the mystery, and the wonderment out of the equation. This is not god-like; this is egocentric.

The Mauthe Family

The Franciscan novices, including Fr. Mauthe (second row, left-hand side)

A long time ago, I heard this ostensibly Native American belief, which proposes that we are not human beings on a spiritual path, but spiritual beings on a human path. And it makes sense. Our spiritual life is an endless continuum, constantly unfolding and revealing itself. As we pass through the valleys and climb the mountaintops of our lives, we are constantly faced with situations that require honesty and unvarnished, earnest introspection. Therefore, being open about our confusions, reconciling what does not add up, and working through the problems and contradictions, even as we accept that we lack some answers, is the only certain way to stay strong and devoted, and to find God.

My inability to feel free to deepen my faith and my relationship with God, on my own terms within the confines of the Franciscan Order, now seems like a divine plan—indeed it was—and I have no regrets about any of it. My period with the Capuchin Friars was a period of great importance to me, and many of them are still my close friends. I also always carry the Order of the Franciscans around me and within me—in my heart, and in my thoughts, as well as in my lifestyle, the simplicity by which I live.

Today, after all these years, I have acquired a degree of wisdom, acceptance, and even appreciation for all that transpired with the Capuchins. However, back then, I was quite disillusioned by the entire experience. Not only did I think that God had tricked me into following his path, and then rejected me, but this had happened twice in a few very short years. Perhaps our dance had to be entertained in some other way? Perhaps I had to live out my life as God's servant in another way, and maybe the priesthood was not for me? I was very young back then, only beginning to know myself and know God, and quite unsure about many major things: myself, where I was meant to go, the world at large, and I definitely had no idea what was yet to be. All this just fueled my disillusionment, enhanced my anxiety about the future, and prevented me from seeing the larger picture. This was a hiccup in my journey, but my life was far from over. I had a lot of possibilities before me. Thankfully, during this time—indeed, ever since—I was surrounded by several wonderful people who were able to console me, guide me, and then nudge me in the right direction. Obviously enough, their suggestion and my solution was to go to college. And so, this is how my brief stint with the Franciscans came to an end, and the new chapter with the Jesuits began.

The next step in my journey took me to Marquette University in Milwaukee where I studied philosophy and sociology. I was always interested in how people got to be who they are and what moved them to operate the way they do, both individually and as a society. At this point, I honestly thought that, after all, I'd end up a doctor or a lawyer, and I had qualifications to go either way. And in those post-war days in the 1950s, the economy was booming, jobs were abundant, and a quality life was within the reach of university-educated people.

Marquette also gave me an opportunity to have new experiences. Convinced that my prospects as a priest had ended at the doors of the Franciscan Friars, I sought new friendships, went out, attended dancing parties, and appreciated all of the lighter, social sides of life. I also continued my long-lasting love with tap dancing. As a youngster, I had developed a love and some skill for tap dancing, and I'd travel around Wisconsin to perform and compete. It was wild! By the time I was in college, I taught others how to dance—for a fee. A guy had to make a living somehow! It was spectacular, and just thinking about it now makes me feel the urge to get on my feet and make some moves.

During this period, I also felt free to enter the dating life too. My call to service had always been a primary motivator for me, and I only rarely entertained the idea of a romantic life. But now, I felt free to experience this side of lay life, too. Unlike my peers who spent prior years thinking (if nothing else!) about their potential relationships, wrestling with desires of heart and flesh, and sharing their experiences with

one another, I was almost like a baby giraffe: confused, innocent, and not exactly able to stand on my own feet. This was
when she showed up, my first romantic love. She was beautiful, charming, and smart, and her wit and her goodness
were enchanting. She had the drive for a great life, too, and
college was only the first step in this promising, marvelous
journey. Unlike me, she was certain of her future. Yet, she
saw something in me and we hit it off. We spent a lot of time
together. We laughed, went to the dances and to the movies,
and had many wonderful, inspiring conversations. Eventually, I fell in love. It was burning, it was powerful, and it was
deep. We even got engaged. It also began my understanding of what it meant to fall in love, to be in love, and to stay
in love—forever. Those were exciting, extraordinary, awe-in-
spiring, and also challenging and confusing times for me.
There was a lot to contemplate, and little time to do so.

Looking back at this time in my life, decades later, it is
obvious that God had a different plan for both of us, and
I cannot help but think that it was His hand that guided
us both to seek out what was best for us. This, of course,
meant that our paths diverged deep into the woods, and
our dance concluded not long after our meeting. However, something we gave to each other—a glimpse of love, a
moment of tenderness, and a deep appreciation—rendered
us both transformed. This special imprint endured many
decades later, too.

In fact, nearly fifty years later, I was down outside
Madison, Wisconsin, preaching for the Children of the
World—a wonderful nonprofit organization that helps
orphans find a home and which I was involved with until
recently—when a woman came up to me, with a mischievous
smirk and a twinkle in her eye, and said, "Hello, good
lookin'!" I was astonished and speechless! It was her—my
first love—after all these years! As I gave her a hug and
looked at her, both of us now significantly older and with
a lifetime of experiences and stories to tell, I still felt a

profound love for her. All of a sudden, we were transported back to that library at Marquette, the decades that had separated us washed away in a moment, and we stood there, two young and hopeful creations: once in love, always in love.

I am still in love with that girl, and I always will be. That's how our life, a lover's dream, is meant to go. Once those profound words are uttered, the responsibility of loving does not ever go away. The reality of our individual journeys saw our roads diverge and our shared story end, but the experiences we had together and the love we had professed for each other never ceased to exist. There's an old saying that everything can be taken away from us except that which we have willingly given to each other. That stays with us forever. I agree.

The experience of falling in love in this way and with this person, back in college, most definitely deepened my spiritual and human experiences. I saw life in a new light. I also understood love in a different, more authentic, more moving manner. This wasn't only during our courtship, but long after it, too. I had assumed to know what love is before, but now I had a clear appreciation of its purpose and its possibility. I was now liberated to experience love in the deepest of ways, and this freedom allowed me to use love—the act of seeking it, receiving it, and giving it—as a motivator behind all I did. It came into a clear view that love was the last and most important ingredient which was missing, if only in my own psyche, in my quest to find myself, my purpose, and then to endeavor to fulfill it. This encounter face-to-face with love jolted me into action, allowing me to recognize the enormity of it, the possibility of it, and its promise as well as my own. It helped me better understand the failings and the wounds of the past. The enormity and sublime promise of love also gave me a way to cope, move forward, envision and create something new, contribute, and in doing so, eventually thrive.

Graduating from Marquette

We need not only fall in love, in a traditional sense, with another human being; there are many ways to love. Love is not the infatuation or a brief encounter with another person; it goes beyond that. Love means to act without prejudice and with your whole heart. It is not dependent on the deeds of another person, or life's circumstances; it is solely dependent and driven by our inner feelings.

You may say, to love earnestly is to also live fully.

In most faith traditions and life philosophies, as well as in all cultures, love permeates the discourse. It is, indeed, the highest emotion of them all. In Christianity, we are blessed with having love play the focal point in Jesus' teachings, exemplified through his words and deeds alike. According to the Gospel of John, we are not only called, but *commanded* to love one another, as the highest aspiration and the noblest endeavor, and certainly most pleasing to God. Since those days of my encounter with romantic love, I have always tried to love unconditionally and indiscriminately. It matters not where we come from, how we live, or whom we love. What matters is that we do.

THE ULTIMATE CALL

This newly found inspiration created a desire to engage more fully with the people in my life and the work I was going to do, but it did not change the fact that I was still utterly confused about my future. How was I going to spend my life? How was I going to contribute to society? I was getting an excellent education, but what was I going to do with it?

Whatever my desires were, for some odd reason I thought little about the legacy I might leave, or the impact I might conjure through my deeds. My mind and my heart were wrestling with who I was and what path I was to take. I had myriad questions, but few answers.

Priesthood, however, was not one of them anymore. Having been rejected twice, once by my own choosing and the other time by the choices of other people, I was quite certain that priesthood was not going to be my future. But then, on one fortuitous day during my senior year at Marquette, at a retreat facilitated by a Jesuit priest and spiritual director, Fr. George Ganss, S.J., fate struck and I came face to face with the Almighty:

"What is your final destiny?" Fr. George asked.

"Are you here about your final destiny and what is that?

Are you going to be an architect, an engineer, a physicist, a philosopher, a politician? Ask yourself, and draw the line to the end: Where do all these things take you?"

I thought to myself, "The End?"

But then it came, "What is beyond the end?" Fr. George asked. "Where do we go after all this is done? What difference have you made when everything's said and done, when the line hits the end, and you have used up this one precious life of yours?

"Where do you go when the ink is gone?"

His questions jarred me. My focus shifted from the earthly questions to the eternal. The eternal world was the one I did not, and perhaps still don't, understand. All we see is what is before us, these three dimensions, but there must be something beyond it—and, if so, what is that?

What was I ultimately going to do that would have the ultimate consequence, that would achieve maximum good? Fr. George required each of us at the retreat, about forty guys, to think about our reason for being alive and what we were going to do to contribute while we are here. This was perhaps the first time that I seriously, comprehensively, and deeply interrogated what each of my imagined callings would entail; his questions inspired me to follow the line to the end, and not stop at the achievement of being called a lawyer or a doctor, but consider what type of a life I would live, what questions I'd continue to answer, and what contributions I might make in exchange for this life.

And so, as I considered becoming a lawyer, I contemplated the realities of an attorney's life, including the numerous injustices I might face and have to be a part of when dealing with the imperfect judicial system; the more I thought about it, the more I realized that becoming a lawyer was not something I felt called to do. I contemplated the callings that had been inspired by my parents—what if I became a chemist like my father? But even if I had been the best of them all, and reshaped the food industry in the country, for example, the question at the end of the line still remained unanswered: What's beyond this realm? What legacy, what impact will I have left on the emotional well-being of others? I even thought about building a build-ing, like an architect or an engineer might do, but then the best I could do is build it a foot taller than the next guy without any real consequence to the eternal. In the end, I didn't think I would have found satisfaction in any of these; to me, personally something was lacking. I thought about being a teacher, too, but what does a teacher do when a stu-dent dies ... when a person stops learning and decides that ignorance is safer than the pursuit of wisdom? That seemed daunting. And then, what if I were a doctor and healed the sick? That seemed to appeal to me, but I didn't think that I had the stamina to pursue such a path. It's a most awesome path, but not an easy one. I would also rather sooth those on their way to God, and the families and friends who stay behind, heartbroken.

These may seem like excuses for not pursuing a par-ticular career. To me, however, they were most honest considerations of how I truly felt about my capacity and my propensity to pursue any of these paths. At long last, I didn't want to lie to myself, as there was really no use to that back then—or ever, really—because only when we can see with clarity, and with unfiltered honesty, will the ultimate path reveal itself. I wanted to figure it out. None of these callings had the same pull or sense of divine intervention, the same feelings of destiny like the priesthood did, so they all ulti-mately faded. I was not excited about any of them. They just didn't feel right.

It was at this moment, by God's grace, that I first con-templated whether priesthood was still an option. Maybe because I was looking at the priest who had asked the ques-tions—the same questions I had asked myself, and would have liked to ask others, too—or because I thought he had some answers to my deepest yearnings, or maybe because I wanted to continue my conversation with God and to seek to understand that which is beyond the earthly realm, or maybe I was not ready to give up, and my inner persistence pushed me to march ahead. It suddenly dawned on me that maybe things didn't work out with my previous avenues to priesthood, but not the priesthood itself. Fr. George was instrumental in helping me come to this realization. In retrospect, he read me like an open book, agreed with my analysis, wholeheartedly, and encouraged me to pursue prieshood. He agreed that indeed this was my calling. No ifs, ends, or buts!

Looking back, I find this entire exercise humorous because my calling as the son of the Church and the servant of God, the faithful seeker of the divine truth, and the one who comforts the afflicted among our brothers and sisters seems to have always been a part of me, and a rather clear prospect all along. Sure, things had not worked out exactly as I had hoped, but this is true many times in our lives: we just don't get what we want when we want it, and in a fashion we had conceived. That does not mean that we should not keep pursuing the things that seem so right to us, however difficult or challenging. A wise fisherman knows there's more than one way to catch a fish, and if my earlier attempts didn't work out, the idea isn't to give up but to find a different way. A failure is only a failure if we give up.

But back then, I guess, I needed that faithful day to stop me in my tracks, and to allow me to hear the call more loudly and clearly than ever before. A great many, far more successful and esteemed religious men and women than me, have had their own versions of this call, arrived through far more exciting and dramatic revelations. Mine was pretty dull, in a dated conference room at Marquette University. Nevertheless, it was a call—simple and quiet, delivering immense joy and putting me on a path that has been unique, exciting, and immensely rewarding . This journey that has tested me, built me, and taught me new ways of love, how

to bring about love in my own life, and how to cope with the lack of love by giving it.

Eventually, after graduating from Marquette, I spent four years at the St. Paul Seminary in Minneapolis earning a degree in theology, after which I was ordained a Catholic priest in the Diocese of Green Bay. It was a long time coming, but it seemed that a turbulent journey had come to an end. New doors to a peaceful, purposeful, clear existence were opening to me. I was overjoyed.

But then, as it often does even when we least expect it, life happened.

OVERTURE

The day I gave my life to serve the Church, my mother, at the age of fifty-one, dropped dead at four o'clock in the afternoon. Just as I climbed the hill, crossing the highest peak, I found myself sliding deeply and rapidly into the abyss of sadness and profound discomfort. And I remember asking God, "How many times are you going to leave me an orphan?" I was devastated. Onnie had been my rock, and her departure deepened an already persistent void.

As the old adage purports, when it rains, it pours. This incredibly shocking and painful loss was followed by a series of rejections, all of which reminded me of my earliest and deepest wound: the rejection of my birth mother. I knew then, just as I know now, that whoever you are, whatever you are, wherever you are, and whatever you need: you are it. You and your God. He is not my last catch, he is my only catch. There are many wonderful people in our lives who willingly travel alongside us, but all roads start and end with ourselves and our God. Without faith in both, we are lost. It is only through this faith that we can seek and find acceptance for the ebbs and flows of life, make sense of them, get off the ground and keep moving even when doing so seems impossible, and embrace responsibility for our own well-being as the primary, fundamental block before we can help others build theirs.

Knowing all this, however, does not change the fact that it is incredibly difficult when you feel that there aren't many alternatives in this life, in practical terms, and that fateful summer proved to be incredibly and—it seemed—unendingly trying.

My adoptive parents were a real gift, and I can't think of biological parents being more exciting than those two people were, particularly my mother. She was an avid reader, and every night since I was a little child, when I could sit up and listen, she'd read books to me or tell me what she was reading. I'd sit on the floor with my shoulders against her knees, her hand scratching my head or back, and I listened, taking it all in. We'd go from history to philosophy to engineering to poetry to science to every kind of thing, and she'd imbue me with what the wisdom and the knowledge was that came out of those passages. I was exposed to all kinds of authors and writers and philosophers at an early age. And my mom, being a religious convert—and having gone through a change from being a strict Lutheran to becoming a Catholic, against all odds with her family—was a woman of great wisdom.

As she was emotionally inclined to view life with a sense of feeling, my father was a scientist who was there with his accuracy. When he weighed paper coming to the mill from Canada in winter time and the pulp was wet, he had to know how much it weighed, how much it lost in its moisture, how much it gained, and what to pay for it. When my dad retired from Kimberly-Clark, he was replaced by Ph.D.'s who'd call him on a consistent basis and ask, "Ray, how do you do this," and sometimes he even had to go down to the mill and actually show them. He was a self-made man, a good scientist, even though he only had a sixth-grade-level education. He knew what he needed to do with his job, and he did it—all with a sliderule, too.

Losing my mom was one of the hardest feats, but drawing on the mixture of my parents' characters and the wisdom they had imparted upon me, I committed to being my own net, doing what I thought was right, and making decisions in accordance with my conscience. I trusted that each road would lead to another, and that each small decision would be a part of a bigger picture.

This was very scary, though, because the only thing that validated me was myself. In life, we look to get a rubber stamp on ourselves and what we do, and when someone disagrees with placing it there, that's where and when we can feel rejected, question ourselves, and feel anxious. And so, as I wrestled with external circumstances and struggled with internal turmoils, everything unfolded as it should.

After my ordination, I was first assigned to serve along a priest at St. Mary's Parish in Peshtigo, Wisconsin, who upon our arrival told my father and I to go right back home to Kimberly. "I don't want you here for the summer," he said. Confused, I explained that Bishop Stanislaus Bona had sent me a letter appointing me to this location for the summer. I guess he did not have room for me in the rectory. His housekeeper had also died that spring and he didn't know how to cook for two people. Thankfully, he told me that I could come up on the weekends. I was expected to arrive at eleven o'clock on Saturday and out of there by early Sunday morning. "You take the confessions in the afternoon, eat supper, hear the confessions in the evenings, and two morning masses on Sundays, and then you are done," he told me. I felt neither here nor there, but something, as they say, was better than nothing.

Then came the end of August. In those days, religious appointments were very, very secretive things. Nobody knew. There were no committees that would decide placements and then leak decisions beforehand. The bishop personally made all the decisions. In my case, the bishop had sent me a letter assigning me to Fr. Vospeck (I think was his name) in Little Chute, Wisconsin. But, truth be told, Fr. Vospeck and I did not agree on much; there was God and all men died, but after that we had nothing in common. And since he already had three assistants, two of whom were my friends, I had spent a lot of time in that rectory and we were well acquainted. So, unsurprisingly, after he found out that I was assigned to him, Fr. Vospeck in no uncertain terms told the Bishop that he didn't want me.

In those days, after the appointments were made, the phones would go wild on Fridays: everybody was calling everybody to share the good news. Everyone knew about the assignments for all eighteen guys by Friday evening, two days before it would be announced in the paper. Therefore, armed with the news, Fr. Vospeck must have called the bishop right away to protest my appointment, because it was early Sunday morning, while I was at Peshtigo finishing up the morning mass, when the phone rang; it was the bishop. He gave me the official notice of Fr. Vospeck's rejection: he didn't want me.

I was hurt. They were virtually extending me an invitation to leave the priesthood, and I considered it. It pressed on the much deeper wound. Not only had I been rejected by the Capuchin Friars, and had just lost my mom, but this was the second priest in a single summer who didn't want me and not because I couldn't do the job, but because of who I was and the ideas I espoused. Never tested, never tried, I was not even given the opportunity! I was deeply angered at what I viewed as a profound injustice. Of course, my own inner emotional turmoil only exasperated the pain. And yet, this was not the end of it. I was still a Diocesan priest though, and something, was going to happen. The bishop told me to come see him on my way home to Kimberly.

When I arrived later that morning, a nun came to the door, not the Bishop, and handed me a letter from him.

The letter said I was going to the Ss. Peter and Paul Parish in Green Bay. An assistant there had back surgery, and I was a fill-in.

All this time, everybody was making decisions about my freaking life except for me. It was crazy. Some people also looked down on me because of my Capuchin experience, which wasn't fair but it was my reality. And, early on, I realized the extent that politics existed within the Church, all the liking and disliking based on personality, and not on one's ability to perform. Meritocracy did not matter. Even my time at Ss. Peter and Paul was temporary, and—for a moment—I wondered, again, whether I should be in the religious business at all. I wanted to serve my Creator, not deal with a bunch of inflated—and insecure—egos. I thought we were better than the perceived "cutthroat" corporate world we were shown on television. My hope, however, didn't change the reality. Where do you go when you are caught up in the middle of all this; where do you find some solace? There weren't many places, but I did have one major source of strength to cling to: God.

In my years at Ss. Peter and Paul I lived with sixteen different priests in the Rectory. There was a pastor and three live-in local priests. On the weekends, one Norbertine priest was brought in to help out because we had a mass upstairs and one downstairs: at 9:30 a.m., 10:30 a.m., and 11:30 a.m. This was my opportunity to meet and get to know some Norbertines. They'd be assigned to us for these weekend duties and stay for a year, a couple of years, or even several years, and in the course of this time I got to know them all. All of them were teachers at Premontre High School or at St. Norbert College, comprising every field: from mathematicians to writers. It was a delight to speak with them about what we were seeing and what was happening. I vividly remember Saturday nights, after confessions had been celebrated, when Fr. Jerome Tremel, O.Praem., a Norbertine priest and later the abbot of the St. Norbert Abbey, and I would get together in my room and talk about what we both were reading, what we thought the needs in the community were, and how we, as priests, might meet them.

In those days, unfortunately, if you were a pastor, you alone were the deciding voice on everything. The rest of us were rarely included in the parish meetings, and we wouldn't really know what was on the agenda, what was discussed, or even if their decisions were meeting the needs of our parishioners that we saw daily as part of our ministry. It was the pastor who signed the checks, not us, and there was a culture of "non-speaking," a painful silence, so we were not to comment on anything. This was neither democratic nor helpful, much less empowering, but the structures were clear.

I recall one Sunday having to preach about the parish picnic that came up the following Sunday. I decided to do it honestly and address the issue we had discussed the Sunday before: no shopping on Sabbath. There was a big debate about people shopping on Sundays, but it did not seem there were any issues with people partying it up on the holy day of rest. So, my way of addressing this conundrum was to say that, just because you put a cross in front of something it does not make it a Christian activity. People may not be shopping, but they are drunk by five in the afternoon. How does that work, how is that just? Needless to say, my approach did not sit well, and I had a "finger-wagging" talk; what I talked about was not on Pastor's agenda.

This was frustrating and reflective of a bigger issue that if it belongs to the Church, or it is done by the Church, it must be right. While I tried to go along with everything (or almost everything) that was asked of me, this was an absolute irritant. I had issues with all this being imposed on me, of course, but my deeper concern was the question of justice. If something is done by the Mother Church does not automatically mean it is right. The history of the Church is ritc with stories of misjudgement and abuse. My goal was not to take authority away from the powers that be, but make sure we served our people in a just, compassionate way, and remained consistent with the changing times and the changing needs of our flock. What worked a thousand years ago may not, and often does not, work today. If we do not adapt, even while staying true to the essential teachings of the church, we will become irrelevant.

That deeply worried me then, and continues to worry me today. It is not, and should not be about a policy; it should be about the people.

My views seemed out of this world for many, so they worked hard to limit my access to opportunity even more. As for me, a chance to do something different, something where I felt I could contribute more earnestly, was a dream. I began to contemplate what that might be. An assignment at a remote parish? I didn't know. I just knew that the politics within the organization were killing my soul instead of stoking my passions and allowing me to get closer to both God and the parishioners I loved and served. I needed space to be impactful. Therefore, I remained disciplined and looked for opportunities, even part-time gigs, to escape the politics and bickering, and seek a place that would afford me a degree of freedom.

Very unexpectedly and quite extraordinarily, this opportunity came in 1961 when Bishop Bona assigned me to the Newman Center at the University of Wisconsin-Extension in Green Bay. I was thrilled, and this is where my interfaith journey began in earnest.

I didn't know much about John Cardinal Newman, nor was I familiar with the other Newman Centers around the country, but we were living at the time of great changes, and the opportunity to build a new program that would impact an entire generation was enthralling. What began as a simple Catholic ministry on campus during the heady, exciting days of Vatican II that brought a powerful sea change to the Church, rapidly expanded to include all God's children as the needs of our community crystalized. It only made sense. We set off on a remarkable journey, and as I sit here, many decades later, I feel very grateful to have had this opportunity. Things like this come to us once in a lifetime, and I was ready to seize it.

From the beginning of my priestly journey, including through the times of rejection and disillusionment, I always wanted to be a faithful and honest servant, and do what the bishop asked me to do. Of course, each bishop saw my individual role and that of the Newman Center (and later the Ecumenical Center) from their own vantage point; they all had their opinions of what the Center was about and how to run it. Through it all, I tried to strike a balance, serve as well as I could, meet the needs of students in the best possible way for them, and yet honor the bishops while leaving my own mark. This was a hard balance, but I always tried to keep it, because I never forgot the freedom and empowerment that came with this job, and direct and profound impact we were making on the lives of those whom we served. We were driven by forces larger than ourselves, and looking back now, it is clear how the winds of change were unstoppable.

I am glad we chose to embrace them.

THE STAGE

To understand the forces that drove me, and others, into the hands of ecumenism, you have to understand the world we were living in. Two words: confusion and tension. The timeless world order we knew so well suddenly experienced a shock, a shift, and no longer was there any order—the world was experiencing massive changes.

After our victory in World War II, the capture of Germany and Japan, and the world dominance that we took on (or, at least, sought after), the United States became the epitome of what the world was supposed to be like without any kind of comparison. As we wrestled to maintain our leadership in the world, setting an example to dozens of other countries that struggled with their own self-determination and internal organization at the sunset of colonialism, we also experienced three competing, but interconnected revolutions at home: economics, demographics, and civil rights. It wasn't a matter of changing one thing at a time, but all things at once.

As our abundant growth ensued, prevailing attitudes about women, minorities, and other nationalities and their influences were called into question. The arrival of millions of immigrants, hoping for a better life, changed the makeup of the United States and infused our culture with richness that was both beautiful and different. The racial discord and disputes, so prevalent for decades, came to a head as people of all colors, rightly so, sought equal treatment. Women also spoke up, seeking a place at the table which was, for most of our country's history, reserved only for men. And, finally, the massive economic changes that drove our awesome affluence fueled much of these social changes. Education and self-reliance became a reality for a lot more people, prosperity was the norm for more people than ever before, and the promise of a better, more self-actualized life was within reach.

Improved civil rights, robust immigration, and a thriving economy were the things that made America better, more authentic, and more honest to its founding principles. But like any change, these transformations were also difficult. They sometimes created unintended consequences, such as the income disparities between various groups, or the over-valuation of certain things and undervaluation of others. This contradiction seemed especially stark. Additionally, some people believed themselves superior, even above the law, and often rushed to maintain the old system through unquestioned obedience to unspoken rules and traditions. Others challenged them. Together, they formed a hodge-podge of confusion and blurriness.

For many of us, these changes were scary at times. The launch of Sputnik in 1957 and the so-called Space Race that ensued only added more uncertainty to the brewing Cold War with the Soviet Union. The fear of a nuclear war was real; these bombs weren't firecrackers and if an artificial comet is up in space, it can also fall to the earth leading to our demise. Any sense of solidarity we felt with the Russians during the war had now evaporated—they were a total stranger, vastly different from us—and the prospect of an all-out nuclear conflict seemed not only possible, but probable. The assassination of John F. Kennedy in Dallas in 1963 only reinforced these fears.

A lot of what was happening at the time seemed out of our control. Many embraced these social changes as long overdue; others viewed them as harmful and resisted them mightily. When we look back at those days, we often remember them with nostalgia and fondness: the fear of a nuclear war never materialized; people within our society gained greater rights and legal protections, however imperfectly; and, the booming economy enhanced the lives of most. But, in those days, the divisions were powerful and the tension unquestionable. Doubt was pervasive, and trust was a rare commodity.

Just like the United States and the Soviet Union struggled on the macro-level, regular people experiencing these enormous changes struggled on a personal and interpersonal level: which ideas and whose ideas were better? How should we live? Whom should we trust? What is right and what is wrong? These questions are so relevant again in today's increasingly hostile and harmful political climate. Of course, the only way out is through common ground. It was in the midst of this ever-changing climate that some of us sought to find a new way by identifying common ground through which we could see each other as friends rather than enemies and recognize the goodness of our fellow humans. It was a matter of getting back to the basics, to the idea that a handshake can mean a lot, that we can doubt what needs doubting but still have the capacity to trust. Our quest was not to recreate what once was—that would mean resisting the change that was inevitable, and, besides, plenty of people were doing that—but rather, to take what once worked and apply it within the present context.

Another big change during this time was the rise of individualism in every sphere of life: religion, commerce, government. All of it shifted from "us" to "me," yet, everyone still sought a sense of unity. So the question then became, how do we encourage people to be the best they can be, in their own right, while still coming together with others for the sake of common good and to fulfill our inner yearning for community? How do we bring those estranged, segregated, and rejected by the forces of ancient beliefs, religions, socioeconomic status, and politics into the fold of mutual respect, justice, and peace? We are all one in the eyes of God, after all, and the journey starts and ends with people's hearts.

In setting up the ministry at UW-Extension, and later at UW-Green Bay, I looked for ways to change people's hearts. If I can change your heart, even turn the edge of a page, moving you from a place of hating to a place of loving, from a place of hurt to a place of healing, I will have ultimately made a tremendous change in the world.

This is what became important to me. I cannot come up with any scientific discovery for the science department out there, I told myself then; I cannot come up with any outstanding pieces of literature for the language department, or lead the sports teams to championships, but what I can do is affect a total package of everybody there, every student and faculty and staff who is willing to live with a little rub off from each other. If all we can do is engage deeply from a standpoint of loving kindness and celebrate our unique differences that would be fine, because no other institution on campus was doing that.

As we set up our shop, first as a small room in the basement, and then an entire building, more and more people seemed to gravitate to us. We were offering what they yearned for: clarity, simplicity, and love. These were the 1960s. External threats and internal discord spurred many people to seek a place where they could meet each other as a community, without judgement and with opportunities for connection.

Driven by a thriving and ever-growing industry, the academic departments were focused on producing a workforce that would sustain such an enormous growth. The industrial machine always hungry for productive citizens contributed to this, as well. If a company wanted a chemist, they'd call out to the university and say, I need a chemist. They didn't care if the chemist was a scientist at heart, versed in Shakespeare, or knew the difference between right or wrong; they needed a chemist who could do the job. What happened to the kids outside of their place of employment wasn't as important to a system hell bent on American productivity and progress, progress, progress! Our university, and all others across the country, complied by offering top-notch training. Education became evermore specialized. This was an opportunity for us, and we too found a specialized niche: we would fill in the gap in the spiritual and personal development of our students. But we first had to build it, and this wasn't going to be easy.

First of all, we were building something entirely new in the community, a religious ministry on a public campus. Second, in addition to figuring out the spiritual aspect of our program, we also had no money to invest in it, as Bishop Bona told me in no uncertain terms early on. "Go out and get the money," he had said. So I found myself, a young priest ordained for only a couple of years, out in the worlds of business, banking, and politics, learning how to rally the support of influential community leaders.

When you look for backing, there's a lot of money out there. If your cause is conservative enough, you'll find more money than you need. But if you come out there with an idea that is more progressive, as my ideas were at the time, this becomes more difficult. The Greatest Generation was beaten into the "old style," but I didn't want the old; I wouldn't accept the old. I wanted innovation, and so did my audience, the so-called Baby Boomers. College students were eager to ask questions and create a new world order that would be more in line with the changing times we were living in.

Furthermore, the Second Vatican Council, which opened in 1962 and was focusing on the Catholic Church's relationship to the modern world, was a great example of the Church adapting to the changing times, and taking the initiative to serve its flock in a way they most needed. But even as the official Church sanctioned it, those of us on the ground trying to implement a different approach still encountered resistance. I ran against the grain of the establishment, while the orthodoxy were scared to ask deep questions, believing that, by doing so, they would endanger their adherence to the teachings of the Church. Perhaps they were simply afraid of change, using the sanctified teachings as a means to cling to the old, to the familiar, to the comfortable, and perhaps as a shield from the rest of us who were laboring hard to affect real change.

Or, for the more thoughtful ones, their resistance was rooted in their inability to adapt, even if perhaps they recognized that there was no other way. History is riddled with examples of institutions that died because they couldn't adapt, but we often forget the lessons of history when we are the ones needing to learn from it. Lastly, there were those whose sheer rigidity of belief, feeling, and thought made them enemies of anything other than their own way of thinking and being. We still have those kinds of people in the world, abounding with their conviction that their way is the only way.

In all of this, our purpose was not the survival of the Church as an organization, but the faithfulness in following the path to truth. The world had changed, people needed something new, on their way to God, and it was our job to provide that. It does not matter which road we walk, or the kind of a bridge we build, as long as there is one to take people to their Creator.

In many ways, and from this writing, you may say I am a relativist, and, to me, the truth is only absolute within the proper context. A different context often means different conclusions. I am a relativist; at the same time, I also have powerful dogmatic lines that close in. And, inbetween, I am a romantic.

This personal makeup begs the question: Can you possibly think all this *and* be a believer? After decades of contemplation and experience, I unequivocally say: of course you can! By the way, this doesn't mean I am a hallmark by which to judge yourself, but certain things just don't fit for me. Some stuff doesn't make sense, and to say it does when it doesn't would be deeply troubling. For me to stand up and propagate that I believe in a particular myth when I don't, I just won't. That would be dishonest, and if I am found of this dishonesty, I would have shaken the faith of those who were listening. In doing so, I would be neither a good theologian nor an effective pastor. Nothing to say of divisions, distances, and mistrust we create between each other when we pretend to not have the same doubts and same questions.

When you are in a position of moral authority, you have to keep course even at those times when you disagree personally, because you cannot come across as duplicit. At the same time, you need not be dishonest. If you have questions, but haven't found enough evidence for your answers, you can live the questions out—this will bring you closer to others and, ultimately, to God. On the other hand, if people are unsure of what you believe in, or your "belief" seems dishonest, how will they know what they ought to believe?

Ultimately, all of us have to follow our heart and our conscience. It is a very interesting thing, how you put together self-revelatory things and truths to which you're exposed, because sometimes they're not the same thing. Sometimes, one has to take prominence over the other. By some standards, for example, I would be thrown out of the Church. By others, I am highly revered. Regardless of any of that, I am a firm believer that contradictions are avenues to truth. Entertaining questions, instead of blindly following, allows us to look for evidence for the things we believe in; things that will throw us off-balance or push us through. This approach leads us to true faith: truth that makes sense to us, is informed by our experiences and our knowledge, and we can freely take ownership of it.

There's a wonderful opera, and in one part of it there is a scherzo during which see-through drapes are put on the altar, and you watch at it as if you're looking at a moving tapestry. Everyone on the stage has a certain mystique, as if dancing behind a smoke screen, and from one moment to another, you see the story reveal itself while, at the same time, a finger is pulling the curtain away, and at that very moment you begin to panic and wonder whether to believe the reality you see or the reality hiding behind the pulled curtain. Which one is real? Which one is true?

Life is very similar. What is its flow? Is it a set of short, intermittent pictures or is it a movie? I don't entirely know if it can be captured in a single, simple truth. I am hoping to find out, somewhere between now and the question mark point when I die. But I firmly believe there's an ending, and a judgement, and a reward, and a punishment. Whatever you name it, or whichever faithful path you use to get there, if you're honest in your heart, when you pray to whatever is supreme to you, you will ultimately reach that destination of truth.

We often conflate religion and faith. You can tell me how many people have joined your church, but you can't tell me how many people have faith. People may come to church on Sunday for for political, marital, neighborly, cultural, and all kinds of other reasons. On Monday, they can switch gods like they might change schools. Therefore, "why" becomes a much more important question. Why do people join churches, then leave shortly thereafter? Either they did not answer "why", they did not answer it fully, or they did not understand the answer. In any case, they did not get to the heart of "why," to the heart of faith, but were stuck at the semantics, the logistics, and the commentary. Or maybe it's the church, and not the people leaving it, which fails to reach the hearts of the faithful and to engage in a relevant way.

I wonder how many people calling themselves Christians know what the differences are between Christianity, Islam, and Judaism? How many people will be able to answer with any honesty if they believe in a Triune God; that is, the Trinity of the Father, and the Son, and the Holy Spirit? And how in three gods being One can there be two natures in Christ, the god-like and the human one?

I was once asked by the Intervarsity Christian Fellowship people on campus to give a talk, but they said before I talked I had to sign some statement. After looking at it, I said to them, "I can't sign this, because it says I believe in God. That's only half of the expression; I believe in God, and a Man, and God-Man."

"So do we," they said.

"But you didn't say that in the statement, so I won't sign the paper," I told them.

It is the questions like this that have intrigued me my whole life. Some people may say that I have left the Church; I haven't. But I am pushing what the Church actually says.

A lot of the world out there is confused by that same stuff, and as I began to build the Newman Center, I was not going to ignore these and similar questions of those eager young minds. Rather, I was going to create a place where we could all safely talk about them, a place that does not indoctrinate, but a space that engages and leaves it free to each and every one of us to find God, and fall in love with God, and rest in Him on our own terms.

After reflecting upon my journey and everything that had transpired up to that point, I came to understand that when you are born on the other side of the fence there is no other way but through it. I often reminded myself to not let the defeatists get me down. As I learned to navigate the difficult waters of those early days, I used to tell myself, "Dick, you are not who you are by choice, you are who you are by God, so be who you are. Don't back down, you don't need to fit into the mold," As noble and heroic as it may seem, going against the grain and affecting change is never easy. Being a rebel is often glorified in our society, but the role isn't for the weak of heart.

Thankfully, my life's experiences up to that point had prepared me for it. I also had the benefit of a very insightful experience, early in my childhood, which helped me commit myself to the cause with all my heart and my soul.

One Mother's Day, when I was in kindergarten, our teacher Ms. Grady had decided to help us make a gift for our moms. She gave us a choice of gray, green, red, or brown clay, and our task was to mix it all up and to put it into a circle, big enough to hold our hand, and then take our right hand imprinted into the clay so you can see every detail. I was so proud of my creation: it was deeply personal, it was creative, and it was for my mom. That afternoon, as my dad came to pick me up, and as I ran towards him enthusiastically to show him what I had created, I dropped the plaque. I started to cry. My dad, being a "true man," told me that it's OK, it's "just clay," and that I could make another one. At that point, having heard my dad's comment, Ms. Grady walked over and explained that I'd never make another one like it in my life. It would never again be the same situation, as I'll never again put the same amount of time, innocence, and love into the project. It will no longer be an original, but a copy.

After hearing her words, I felt better. She understood what I was experiencing, and knew how to put it into words. She also taught me an important lesson: however imperfect something may be, like a clay project of a four-year-old kid or even this book, it is still an original, unrehearsed creation just like each of us is. It does not matter if we can create it more perfectly later—that later opportunity may never even come. What matters most is that we give it our life and our soul in the first place, and do so fearlessly. This applies to everything in life. There are no redos, overdoes, encores, or rehearsals: this is it. It's now or never.

Building the Newman Center, was a chance to endeavor into a new direction. I took the bull by the horns, and ran with it.

THE NEWMAN CENTER

Since the earliest days at the Newman Center, I relished working with young people and engaging them in discussions about philosophy, politics, religion, the meaning of life, and, of course, God. In fact, it was my favorite part of the job. However, this new endeavor put my leadership and business skills to task, too.

In building the Newman Center, I needed the support of the community; I needed wisdom, of course, but I also needed money. And to get it, I established a Board of Directors and invited people from the community to join. If they had agreed to serve, they were expected to contribute at least $100 annually—no small sum in 1961. Our philosophy was that if you wanted to be a part of it, you had to get involved in every way. We built strength through investment.

At first, personal contacts and people directly within the Church stepped up to help out. One name that immediately comes to mind is that of Msgr. Mark Schommer, who served in the Diocesan administration at the time and was one of the first people who contributed quite a bit of his personal money. The Knights of Columbus were instrumental, too, in those early days. They contributed $2 per person in order to help our program, and I don't think we would have made it

Breaking ground for the Newman Center

without them. However, as time went on, and people saw the potential and the sincerity of our effor, others joined in and invested in us, too.

One of my earliest and most fervent supporters in building the Newman Center was Jim Madigan, a young entrepreneur who had just founded *FEECO International* a few years before. As a father of four, Jim was enthusiastic about my efforts, and he and his wife Doris have has been close friends and supporters for over fifty years. He helped open doors in the community and connect me with some of the movers and shakers around town, which allowed me to not only understand who is who in the area but recruit high caliber people to the Board of Directors. Jim's were the first investments in the Center, too, but he never shied away from literally rolling up his sleeves and doing what needed to be done. It was Jim and the late Joseph Van Drisse who, along other Board members and me, one evening, laid out the floor in the first Newman Center on Hartung Street. Such has been Jim's character and our friendship. As for Joe, he and his wife Sarah, and later on their daughter Marianne, have done an incredible amount of good for our community and the world.

Other people on the Board during those early days included Harry Bins, Ray Van Essen, George Ziegelbauer, Gordon Malcore, Elmer Bercaeu, Frank Zeise, William Golueke, Fred Fisler, Dr. George Nadeau, Max Johnson, Joseph McMillan, Walter Dettman, Larry Laes, Mike Van Schyndle, J.J. Welhouse, and Heinz Brummel, all of whom were giants in their own right and essential to our effort.

Before we had the building, however, we had arranged with Ted Savides, the Dean of the UW-Extension Center, to use one of the rooms in the basement during the week. Ted was one of the people very suspicious of our efforts but equally intrigued by the value we'd bring to the students. This one room wasn't enough, though, and very soon I began searching for a way to get a space specifically dedicated to the Newman Center.

The help first came when Fr. John Gehl, the rector at the Green Bay Cathedral downtown, told me about a piece of land on East River that he had acquired to help his parishioner. Apparently, the man was on vacation when his son made a bad business deal, and in order to save the business he needed to sell the land. Fr. Gehl decided to help, but beyond it, he had no idea what to do with the land and, to my delight, was willing to gift it to us.

The land covered a city block on what was then known as the East River Parkway, and it was directly adjacent to the Extension Center. In other words, it had the perfect location for our purposes. But there was little we could do with the land without a building, and we had no money to build one. Then, one day, one of the ladies high up in the Green Bay Catholic Women's Club told me about their building downtown, next door to the *Green Bay Press-Gazette*. The building once served as a place for Catholic girls from rural areas to have a room and a safe place to stay while working in the city during the week, but in recent years they used it only a couple of days a week, and it had become somewhat of a burden to maintain. It also needed a new roof and

Entrance to the completed Newman Center on Hartung Street

major renovations. At the same time, I also learned that the *Press-Gazette*, which was growing at the time, had coveted the building for a while and was willing to give them some money for it. Connecting all these opportunities, I proposed to the Catholic Women's Club to sell the building to the *Press-Gazette*, so that they could build a much-wanted parking lot, and then give me $60,000 to build a Newman Center, and on two afternoons a month, when the Club had their meetings, I'd provide them with a brand new building. This way, everyone gets what they want! After some more wrangling, and a vote by 680 members of the Catholic Women's Club, the plan moved forward: Mrs. Ervin Decker and Mrs. Sylvester Linzmeyer signed on the dotted line, the Club's building was sold, and we got the funds for the Center.

Now that we had the land and the money to build a center, Newman Center's board member Heinz Brummel, a renowned German architect and a good friend, volunteered his time and talent to both design and supervise the construction of the building. He drew up five designs, and after much discussion and paring down, we settled on a simple yet beautiful structure.

The next step was obtaining the building permits, which seemed easy enough except for a little detail I had no knowledge of: this area of the City of Green Bay had been precluded from construction by a law dating 20 years back, and our request was denied. Apparently, sometime in 1942, the City of Green Bay voted to make the East River Parkway restricted for construction, and no house could be sold on either side of the East River except to the City. The City, in turn, could not sell it either because the area was earmarked for a park. Therefore, the piece of land Fr. Gehl bought and then gifted to us had become a part of this East River Parkway and was off-limits to building. Now, all of a

The Newman Center building during the flooding of the East River

sudden—just as we thought we had it all squared away—we had to fight to convince, not only one government body, but two, to take a chance on us and give us an exemption so that we could build.

After discussing the situation with the Newman's Board of Directors, we concluded that we had to go before the City's Parks Commission first, and ask them to review our case, but then instead of denying us, defer our issue to the City Council which, thankfully, they did. Now, we were on the City Council's agenda, and our entire Board of Directors came to lobby our local legislators to grant us a permit and witness the outcome. This was one of those wonderful, teaching moments, when our friend and Green Bay's mayor at the time, Dominic Olejniczak, worked his magic by calling in the "blue chips"—favors from councilmen whom he had helped in the past—to spearhead the issue in our favor. Thanks to his intervention and willingness to use his considerable political capital for our cause, our permits were granted, and we were able to move forward.

This was one of those episodes from my life where a collection of "ifs" unveiled itself in all of its glory. If Fr. Gehl had not purchased the land from his parishioner, we would have had no starting point; if the Green Bay Catholic Women's Club wasn't ready to part with their old building and if the *Green Bay Press-Gazette* wasn't eager to acquire it, we would have had no money to build; if Green Bay's mayor Dominic Olejniczak had not believed in our cause and had not stepped in, we could have never built ... and on and on it goes. Such has my life been, and indeed our human experience, a constellation of ifs ... leading from one crossroad to another.

Building our Newman space was a wonderful experience, an exciting endeavor, and also filled with all kinds of stories. During the construction, I made it a point to be on site all the time in case there were questions to answer or to help in some other way. One day, while observing the activities, I was casually approached by this middle-aged man—whose name I can no longer remember—who was smoking a pipe and seemed quite entertained by our work.

He asked me, "Are you the guy building this?"

"Yes, I am," I responded.

He then proceeded to tell me about the flooding of the East River, which had taken place several years prior, and to warn me that we had to stop what we were building, revise the plans, and build the building higher in order to avoid

future flooding. Conveniently, he also informed me that he had put up a nail into a wood signifying how high the water rose and which could serve as a guiding marker for us.

Thinking that he had nailed a screw into a tree, I asked, "But, how will we know the exact level if this had happened years ago—don't trees grow?"

Calmly, he replied, "Not if they're telephone posts."

We heeded his advice, revised the plans, and built the

A portrait commissioned by Mr. and Mrs. Golueke of Green Bay. Painter: William Juhre

building higher, only to bless him for his advice many times since. It was not long after the completion of the building that the East River flooded, rendering his advice truthful and our building safe. Had it not been for him, and his God-sent message, all of our new furniture and the contents of the building would have been ruined. Talk about serendipity—and the Holy Spirit in action!

Like any endeavor that challenges the old ways and attempts to accomplish something new, building a Newman Center adjacent to a public university became an issue early on. I remember a particularly jarring letter, written by a faculty member in the English department, about the Catholic community building a Newman Center and infusing education with religion. The professor's wish was for the church to stay out of education. What he, and others, didn't understand at the time was that it wasn't the Church that we were trying to instill in the young minds. Rather, we were building something that would offer students a transformative and safe environment to freely ask questions; to learn about themselves, other people, and what it means to serve; to wonder about the possibilities of the vistas beyond this the mundane; to find purpose; to make friends; to seek (and find) God; to nurture a faith life; to fall in love. We were not proselytizing, but merely filling in the gap in the development of the whole person.

In this entire process, I also felt that if we could give even one kid a little light, as they are frightened by the shadows in the dark; if we could quiet their fears, and encourage them to dig deeply within to find strength and courage to be the best they can be, then we have done the world a service. Our goal was to help enrich the experience of students, a dream that still lives on in both word and deed.

Protests against our program from outsiders weren't the only challenges, however. Soon after we began to grow, the bishop informed me that some priests were opposed to my work, and even some parishioners were, too. I guess they were concerned that we'd take the kids out of the parishes. On the other hand, others liked our effort because they didn't have to deal with the eager minds asking too many questions—questions that many priests would rather not even try to answer.

Another vivid opposition that came early on and which has stuck with me all these years, was from St. Norbert College. After my appointment as director of the Newman Center and having followed the bishop's directive to go out into the community to raise funds for our program, I received a letter from Fr. Dennis Burke, O.Praem., president of St. Norbert College, admonishing me for doing so. As the only Catholic college in the area, St. Norbert benefited from the support of men and women who, for decades, contributed thousands of dollars to the benefit of the college and its students. Now, all of a sudden, they told Fr. Burke, there's this young priest at UW-Extension who also needed their support and that they'd be splitting it up. Fr. Burke wasn't happy. At the time, I was quite overwhelmed by the variety of pressures: financial, political, logistical, not to mention a desire to offer ministry in a meaningful and impactful way to my students. His letter only added to the strain. How dare I?

Burke was somewhat of a legend in the community, having been chosen by the founder of the College and the first Norbertine abbot in the United States, Bernard H. Pennings, O.Praem., to lead the College after the latter's death. And he did so marvelously well. He expanded the College substantially, raised quite a bit of money, and was also well-known for his friendships with high profile individuals, such as Vince Lombardi, Jimmy Carter, and even John F. Kennedy, who visited the St. Norbert campus in 1960. And then, there was me, a young Diocesan priest ordained only a few years earlier, challenging—indirectly and unintentionally—what had been a very thoughtfully crafted set-up.

At that moment, one may argue, I was a man with a challenge and no opportunity. Fr. Burke's letter was scathing. I still remember it. Thankfully, having befriended several other Norbertines and in following their counsel, I found a way to respond in a manner that put Fr. Burke at ease and closed this episode. In the end, maybe he understood that I wasn't such a big threat after all, and that our work was worthwhile, beneficial to the students and our community, and maybe even to the world as a whole.

In the face of challenge after challenge, we persevered, and with the new building at our disposal, finally, our work began in earnest. Our programs and weekly services engaged hundreds of students, as well as many members from the wider community. We collaborated with campus departments, organizations in the city, as well as organizations from around the state, including other Newman Centers in Wisconsin. In fact, it would be these early collaborations that would, years later while we were building the Ecumenical Center, help us acquire a stained glass window from the very first Newman Center in the Unted States, located in Madison. The window depicts the finding of Christ as a child in the Temple, symbolizing the innocence in the pursuit of God's love and raw truth. You can still see it at the Center today.

Nevertheless, building our first building, strengthening and expanding our Newman Center, and developing new relationships was only the beginning of what was yet to come. A bigger plan had begun to reveal itself.

UW GREEN BAY

After World War II, a great many soldiers returning from the war and benefiting from the G.I. Bill pursued higher education, increasing the need for colleges and universities exponentially. This was evident in all parts of the country, and Green Bay was no exception. Our UW-Extension Center was working hard to meet the needs of the eager and ever-growing population, but in talking to students daily and observing the tremendous growth in interest and attendance, it became clear to me early on that our community would need a four-year public university. At the same time, the University of Wisconsin was expanding to include two additional campuses, but it was left to the individual communities to advocate to be chosen as the sites for these new campuses. I began to wonder how we could mobilize area's movers and shakers in support of such a wonderful cause, and it was not long after that the opportunity presented itself.

Sometime in 1963, I was invited to give a talk to the Downtown Lion's Club, a fraternal organization gathering many of the leaders in our community. At this meeting, rather than talking about whatever was on the agenda, I was moved to make my case: Green Bay needed a four-year public university. Maybe there was something I had said that inspired those in the audience, or maybe we were all thinking the same thing, but after that night, the community mobilized behind the pursuit of this idea. Our efforts were only strengthened when others spoke and acted in favor of this dream. I remember an article by Ted Savides in the *Green Bay Press-Gazette* whereby he communicated that the current UW-Extension Center would be at capacity by 1965 and predicted that a new university could enroll in upwards of 5,000 students. (As it turned out, years later, Ted's prediction was correct.) These numbers only added urgency to our cause.

What followed were several exciting and anxiety-inducing months and years as Green Bay fought to have a public university in its midst. Every community in the state wanted one of the campuses, and understandably so. Universities, with their faculty, staff, and, of course, their students, infuse tremendous economic growth into a community fortunate enough to have them. They create jobs, ignite youthful energy, attract leading minds from a variety of fields, offer an added—arguably, more enlightened—voice to the community, and often bring national recognition. This is to say nothing of the cultural benefits to the local society. To me, of course, it was about bringing the cultural diversification, nationalities, and personalities of all kinds, and bridging the gaps between seemingly disparate groups through education.

Building a new university in any community is an enormous, even daunting task, but the richness a university brings to a community is unparalleled and well worth the effort. Eventually, it came to pass, by the legislature in Madison, that the one of the two new campuses would be in the Kenosha-Racine area in the southeast part of the state, and the other in the northeast—the Green Bay-Fox Valley area.

This, however, led to a struggle between Brown and Outagamie counties to find a suitable location for the new university. The question was: will it be built in Appleton or in Green Bay? Everyone wanted in on the game, everyone had something to say, but after months of active, deliberate, persistent, and persuasive activity, as well as the promise by Brown County to donate the land, the Wisconsin legislature selected the Shorewood site on the very coastline of the Bay of Green Bay as the chosen location. Everyone in Green Bay rejoiced, except perhaps for a few members of the Shorewood Golf Club who would be affected by this major development. And, of course, everyone in Fox Valley protested. They even challenged the decision through the Wisconsin Supreme Court, but the case was thrown out. The University of Wisconsin at Green Bay (UWGB) would go on to transform the lives of thousands and add an entirely new dynamic to our community's intellectual, cultural, and social fabric.

There's an interesting anecdote about the shrewdness of one man who foresaw the future university and quietly went on to labor to secure the land necessary for its inception. As the story goes, this businessman slowly bought up what was once farmland on the Shorewood site. No one thought much of it, as he endeavored to make purchases through other people too, but eventually, parcel by parcel, he collected several hundred acres making them an ideal site for a university. The entire land was eventually purchased by Brown County and the City of Green Bay, offering a sprawling site for the ambitious project and making good on his investments. This act was authentically Green Bay, a testament to the area's long-lasting business acumen.

After the site was chosen, the land secured, and the date for opening—Labor Day, of 1969—set, this new establishment needed a leader. After an extensive national search, the UW Board of Regents hired Dr. Edward Weidner as the university's first chancellor. Ed was an extraordinary man and a great friend until his death in 2007.

Ed came to Green Bay from the University of Kentucky, where he had served as the director of the Center for

Natural Entrance — Chancellor Edward Weidner looks over the abandoned sand pit that will form a logical entrance to the university site off Nicolet Road. The students and public will enter the main part of the campus through an underground mall that comes out on a cul-de-sac constructed in the excavated pit.

Development Change, and prior to that he was in Hawaii, where he worked as the vice chancellor of the East-West Center's Institute of Advanced Projects at the University of Hawaii.

He was truly a visionary: during his first visit to Green Bay, Ed pledged to build a university like no other in the country, and many—myself included—would agree that he lived up to that promise. Perhaps it was his zeal for innovation that forged and propelled UWGB as the first eco-university in the country, or maybe it was his deep commitment to collaboration that inspired "communiversity." Either way, UWGB grew into a formidable and unique institution of higher education in the United States.

It was not long after he first arrived to Green Bay that Ed and I met and spent several hours together. We spoke to each other about our visions for the university, and the ways we could be helpful to each other. Early on, virtually from the very beginning, we both recognized in each other a kindred spirit. Of course, there was also the mutually-beneficial part of our relationship: Ed needed my credibility in the community to push certain initiatives forward. He had no reason to tell me why he did anything, but he'd spend hours talking to me, partly to share, and partly to justify his decisions. He'd tell me the things he knew I'd understand, but other people might not. He silently wanted me to defend him publicly in the community. Ed was a shrewd man, and he knew that I was surrounded by the kinds of people who would trust my judgement about him and his actions. On the other hand, I needed Ed to support what we were trying to do with the Center. We needed each other. And so it went: meetings, lunches, dinners, and countless phone calls. We used to have this unspoken approach that if he needed something from me, he would call, and then come over to see me; likewise, if I needed something from him, I would head over to his office or we would grab a burger at the Student Union and talk.

Ed did not shy away from expressing his views on any topic, and he had some strong opinions on what our ministry should be about. He was very ecumenical, and very interested in offering students personal and spiritual opportunities for development regardless of who they were or where they came from. Ed's commitment, until the end of his life, was to the university he led from its inception. But his confidence in his vocation as a higher education administrator and a community leader meant that he had the hutzpah to engage with whomever could benefit his university. And so, from the very beginning, he wanted to partake in all that we were trying to accomplish, first with the Newman Center, and then later with the Ecumenical Center. He also encouraged us to be bold and ambitious in raising funds to secure the longevity of the institution we were forging, encouraging and supporting us to do the very same thing he was doing: build for the long run. I especially remember one Ecumenical Center Board of Directors meeting, many years after we met, at which Ed urged us to raise a $1,000,000 endowment for the Center. Many around the table were left speechless, not only because this number in those days—the early 1970s—was daunting, but also because one may argue we'd be competing with the university's philanthropic efforts. Yet, it was that university's chancellor who urged us to undertake this ambitious effort. To Ed, it was not a competition. We were all on the same team, building an environment for students to thrive intellectually, spiritually, and in every other way. Our successes were therefore his success, and vice versa.

This attitude of Ed's was evident right away. It was only two days after Ed arrived to campus, to officially assume his duties as chancellor, that I invited him and Bishop Wycislo to my house for dinner. We spent several hours talking about education. Wycislo was a broad-minded man, exposed to a variety of things and perspectives. While Ed's past experiences made him both open and curious.

We sat in my living room, after dinner, drank wine until 11:30 p.m., and the two of them bonded. The bishop shared with Ed his views on the role the university had to play in our community, and Ed, too, gave his insights on ways in which the Church could help. The two men hit it off, paving the way for a mutually beneficial relationship lasting decades. Within a month, Bishop Wycislo was appointed to the Board of Advisors for UWGB, and I felt elated. I wanted to get things done without a record of it, and in this particular case, I served as a conduit between two powerful men in our community, bringing them together for everyone's benefit.

I have a lot of stories about my time spent with Ed, but my favorite one had to do with our land swap. There were many moving pieces in setting up this new university, and Ed was intimately involved with all of them. One of the biggest, most time-consuming, and challenging tasks was designing and developing the physical plant. The university had several hundred acres at its disposal, and all that land had to be used well. As Ed and his team worked tirelessly to put all pieces together—a process that lasted several years, including a significant time after the official opening—I got a call from him not long after construction got underway.

He went right for it, "I need some land of yours," he said.

I laughed. "How much of the land do you need?"

"In some places it is seventeen inches, and in other places it is forty feet."

Ed was talking about a parcel that would later be known as the "German House," which we as the Center had bought in anticipation of the new university and needing increased capacity to work with students on both campuses—the Extension and the Shorewood. Apparently, his architects assumed the land around the house belonged to the university, so they placed the campus' main entrance there. The plans were drawn up to build buildings and roads, as well as install sewage pipes and electric wiring, and they also very carefully designed the entire campus—for the things that would be built right away as well as for those to come in the years that followed. Going back to the drawing board was not a feasible option—the plans had already been approved, made public, and it would cost a fortune to change them. Besides, the terrain and the logistics made this spot perfect. By the same token, Ed told me, there was no money for land acquisition, either. If he had tried to do anything to reimburse us at that point, he'd end up in the headlines of local and state newspapers. Likewise, I faced the same prospects. If we didn't give up the land, the *Green Bay Press-Gazette* would carry an article: "A priest costs state millions to re-route the entrance." Architects didn't know that was not the university land, and thought they'd be fine, and now I'd be the bad guy. A guy who proposed the university in the first place was now literally standing in its way!

Ed offered to give us some land on the other side of the campus in exchange for giving up our land right now. This seemed like a fair compromise. The Board of Directors and I agreed to it. However, given the location of the new parcel— at the very heart of the university campus, between the athletic center and residence halls—this was not an easy sell either. Ed encountered opposition among his own people, too. They protested, what if Mauthe's folly doesn't live on and they sell it to a brothel, or a bar? What kind of a mark would that leave on our students? With the mix of humor and ingenuity, Ed's response was legendary.

"This just can't happen," he said. "Catholics are involved, and they don't believe in divorce!"

Eventually, the land-swap went smoothly: Ed and the university got the envisioned entrance, and what is now the Mauthe Center received two acres of land right at the heart of the university campus. It was years before we claimed the land for the new building, since we would need money to build it. So, in the meantime, we continued to serve students from our locations on Hartung Street and by the university entrance. The latter spot, became known as the "German House," because we had rented the space to the university for the German Language Department. There was also another small building on this property that the university used for their purposes and paid us rent.

This is how Ed and I dealt with each other; we both had visions for our causes, and they intersected deeply. By working together, we were able to achieve our respective goals and help each other out along the way. This mutual respect, understanding of the other person, and a desire to work together were the hallmarks of our relationship, and also the principles we both tried to instill within our organizations and the students with whom we engaged. Just like our lives were interconnected, so have the lives of our children— UWGB and the Mauthe Center—been intertwined in the closest of ways for over fifty years now.

If all future leaders of our respective institutions embraced even a drop of the desire Ed and I had for working together, and of the respect we held for each other, and of the understanding we maintained for the other's vision, and, ultimately, of the trust we bestowed upon each other, I have no doubt that both brothers, UWGB and the Mauthe Center, will have bright future ahead.

Ed was not the only person at the university with whom I maintained a great relationship. There were many. I fear to mention any particular person and forget someone else, but some names that vividly come to mind include the legendary basketball coach, Dick Bennet, who brought students from far and wide. He understood the value we offered to his athletes, and I understood why sports are important to a university of our caliber—or any university for that matter. Dick and I worked closely for many years, and he served on the Center's Board of Directors. Betty Brown is another person who was an ally and a good friend for many years. She was Ed's secretary, and her husband was an American Baptist, who ran a Baptist church over on the west side.

In fact, it was Heinz Brummell, the architect who designed both the Newman Center and the Ecumenical Center, who also designed and built the Baptist church over there.

Another marvelous person, not only at the university but also in the educational and political life of both Green Bay and the state, is Judy Crain. She is an all-Green Bay girl, whose remarkable lifelong career has made Green Bay better in every way. Everything she has done as a politician and as an educator was for the benefit of others. She contributed her time, talents, and treasure to our work at the Center, too. A remarkable woman, I love Judy like a sister. A couple of other people from the university who were on our board in those early days were Dr. Robert Cook, professor of environmental science, and Dr. Arnold Zander, an instructor of political science, and a very active leader in the social justice causes.

This is to say nothing of the honor, the pleasure, and the humbling opportunity to interact and work with hundreds of faculty and staff members and thousands of students over nearly thirty years in association with the University of Wisconsin. While attempting to recall all of their names would be an enormous task, I do remember them all, and remain grateful for having crossed paths with each and every one of them. They have inspired, challenged, and motivated me in ways that words cannot describe, but emotion remembers. Not all of them agreed with me, or I with them, but I hope that together we made this world better and more beautiful, more colorful and more diverse, and UWGB more special and meaningful to the students whom we served.

Those were the days of great excitement and energy, a zeal for growth and transformation, and service. I vividly remember walking to our first, small room at the Extension Center for our first Newman Center meeting, and then again, several years later, for the laying of the cornerstone of the first UWGB building on what was then known as the Shorewood campus. Then came the days of establishing the UWGB

Committee for Campus Ministry, engaging over a dozen denominations, and building the new Ecumenical Center building, and hosting thousands of students and community members from all walks of life. This work has endured because of the very fundamental commitment each of us shared: caring for one another and for our students, even amid our occasional differences or disagreements.

THE ECUMENICAL CENTER

As early as 1963, if not before, the Newman Center began to attract students from all walks of life—Catholic, Protestant, and Jewish alike—and it only made sense: we were a place for students to gather as they sought to find God and commune with each other. It did not matter to me what their backgrounds were as long as we shared a basic respect for each other, and a sense of openness to those different than us. In time, we would bring together fourteen faith traditions under the same roof, including brothers and sisters from many Christian denominations, as well as from Islam and Buddhism. Although many of us could not exactly put our finger on the deep draw we felt toward those who were outwardly different than us, we all sought and, eventually, found closeness with each other. The spirit of ecumenism began to take place in our community with zest and fervor. And we were not alone in this endeavor.

A great many people around the world were sobered up by the events that had transpired only a couple of decades earlier: World War II, the Holocaust, and the phenomenon in which people of all nationalities, colors, creeds, and backgrounds huddled up together in the trenches, in the basements, in the cafés, and on the streets in order to share with each other, to protect one another, and to be one

Eucharist: a symbol of joy and hope

human family against evil. It did not matter if a person was a Jew or a Catholic or a Muslim or a Protestant or a Buddhist, or had no specific faith at all, during the Blitz, as those bombs fell down to the ground—seeking to kill without mercy or apology—people would lie down, put their arms over each other in the gesture of protection, and pray to the Almighty that they may come out alive. They shared the little food they had, looked after the little ones, exchanged stories and hopes to maintain sanity in the reality filled with darkness, both proverbial and literal, and made bonds out of which their children would learn to come together like never before in the history of the human race.

In those times of utter pain, and danger, as hearts were broken and lives lost, it became clear that no matter who we are, or where we come from, or where we are going—it is our deepest, rawest, most sincere human instinct to see the divine in each other, to help and protect as best as we can, and to love one another as He has loved us. These lessons, proven in times of despair, did not get lost on my generation, or the Baby Boomers, who, in those days, sought a way forward filled with love instead of hate, acceptance instead of rejection, and, as much as possible, and as often as possible, an understanding for the one who in the past may have been estranged, or whom we were taught to view with a dose of fear, suspicion, or uncertainty. The Second World War moved millions closer to each other, and we saw the impacts of this proverbial migration in our daily lives on a college campus in a small Wisconsin community.

A new thread, a new friendship

On the world stage, of course, the Second Vatican Council had commenced in Rome with a goal of renewing the Church, in the spiritual sense, and bringing those estranged from it back into her fold. It was not a matter of bringing people to a particular church, it was the effort designed to inspire and lead people—all people—to the Christian church Jesus spoke about: a Church that does not discriminate and a Church that brings all of God's children under Her roof. This process legitimized people's feelings by introducing the lessons and their sentiment into the institutional structures as a way of expanding, preserving, and even protecting the wonderful wisdom and openness which came on the heels of such horrific events. The idea was that we would not forget, but use the experiences of our fellow kin to come closer.

We were determined that those who died—millions of innocent people who lost their lives in the face of bigotry, hatred, fearmongering, and propaganda—would not have died in vain. This was the spirit that has motivated and inspired us for many decades.

For me, having experienced rejection on various levels in my life, I was determined that no other human being who came before me would ever feel the ire of rejection, and instead experience love regardless of their faith tradition. This commitment was especially intense having lost my mom only several years earlier; hers was the story of rejection too. Having been brought up a strict Lutheran, she caused quite the uproar in her family's circles when she decided to marry my father, a Catholic. They were both, just like my brother, Ed and I, rejected by some who could not see passed their bigotry yet pretended to love us and love God. Likewise, in my priestly ministry, some Catholics urged me to hate Protestants, especially Protestant ministers. But this I could not do: that simply seemed wrong, and furthermore, I was taught differently. I understood that rejection and bigotry goes both ways. If it hurts me, it must hurt the other person, as well. Who am I, then, to impart pain upon another human being, regardless of the path another person is walking? We are meant to love one another. I saw the value of love in the example of my parents, and it only made sense that I would continue on that same path.

Therefore, during that time of ecumenical awakening, understanding how strongly my earliest experiences with rejection had influenced me gave me the strength and the commitment to find those touching points—common origins, common paths—among all who came through my doors. Of course, at times of great change, there are always people whose fear of change drives them to judge, to speak hurtful things, to obstruct, and it was no different in my case. There were people in my surroundings who judged me for engaging with "those" non-Catholics. As time went on, my resolve only strengthened, and my response was always the same:

"I am sorry if this is disagreable to you, but in my soul, everyone who walks through that door is a creation, a masterpiece, and they deserve the same kind of respect and love as you or I do. They're unique, and they're of God, and God makes no mistakes. It is our job to help them become the best version of themselves; the best they can be."

Engaging with UWGB students in conversation

I never was one to encourage conversions, or to pretend my own faith tradition is better (or worse) than any other. It's not a competition. Instead, I wanted people to engage deeply in those philosophical questions, to challenge everything, because only then can they reach their own truth. There is no shame in asking questions and in knowing thyself. Indeed, doing so is essential on our way to God. Therefore, if someone was a Catholic, I wanted them to be the best possible Catholic they could be. If they were a Jew, I wanted them to be the best possible Jew, and so on. The world needs people to come to life, to live fully, and they can only do so when they're allowed and encouraged to be the best they can be—regardless of whether that makes someone uncomfortable or not, or if it is or isn't in accordance with a particular norm. As I always told my students, be an original. Be the best you can be and live a life in a way that there is nothing left in the end—no unaccomplished goals, no unachieved dreams, and no regrets. Reach your best

Bishop Wycislo with Pope John Paul II

potential, and always treat others with respect and dignity; the rest is just commentary.

In a much larger sense, I was driven by love. I wanted to be loved, of course, but I also realized that when we love another human being, we unconsciously liberate them in becoming more true to what is in their hearts and in their true nature. Our love renders them more loving of themselves, including their faults and shortcomings, and more compassionate toward other beings. In doing so, we are putting them on a path to God, without the barriers of our worldly condition, and the inherent imperfections that come with it, and then they're no longer a product of the original sin, but divine creations with a potential to find God's love within themselves and rest in it. Maybe this logic would not, or did not, work for all—but I wanted to try it; I was the one who needed to channel my own need for love by giving it to others—I thought that others would benefit from it. I also wanted them to try it, too, and to give to others.

Together, we were bound to create something powerful.

I also wanted those with whom I interacted to always ask me tough questions, even to challenge me, because wrestling with their queries and searching deeply for answers would make me a better pastor, a better servant of God. It is easy to say, "My book says this, I am right, and you're wrong," and many have stuck to that approach. But it is not always easy to find the patience to try to understand another human being, and to find love for that person even when they seem completely unlike us, or believe things we don't. As long as one's behavior or belief does not directly harm another human being, I am fine with it, and they have a place in our Center. Likewise, someone may be the best Catholic, yet they live out none of these values and fall short of God's directive to "love one another." As authority figures—pastors and priests, rabbis and imams, gurus and monks—it is our job to promote love and peace, even in the face of great opposition, and not only through words but also our deeds.

I remember one year, I had heard about several Jewish students from New York who were staying in Green Bay, so I made a point of engaging with them. They were marvelous young people. And when the Jewish High Holidays came around, I offerred to find local Jewish families that would host them during these holy days. Students loved the idea, so I phoned my friend, Rabbi Isaac VanderWalde of the Cnesses Israel Synagogue in Green Bay, to see if he could help. Isaac engaged the deeply welcoming Jewish community in the area, and each student had a "holiday home." This act of partnership not only provided opportunities for these young people to honor their faith, to celebrate, and to have a home away from home, but it also strengthened our connection and enhanced our collaboration.

Our work was always about the young people whose lives we help shape. By putting them first, by removing our egos that prevent us from seeing God's grace as we endeavor to care for the young people, we are given the opportunity to be more in sync with God, more authentic to our calling, and more charitable, and more loving. In the end, it isn't about some commentary, or who is right and who is wrong, but about the lives we touch, about the lives we impact for the better. Ultimately, it will be those people, whose lives we impacted positively, who will carry on the practice of kindness and charity forward bringing about a better, more peaceful world.

In those days, there used to be these "religious preference cards" that helped us understand where our students came from and what their spiritual needs were. And so, as I became more aware of these needs, I would reach out to various pastors for assistance, as well as to the Brown County Clergy Association, an organization that brought together pastors from various Protestant denominations. Some pas-

Celebrating Mass

tors, as well as some priests, were opposed to our work, while others liked to be able to send their kids to us. They'd rather not engage in the philosophical questions of the "new generation," but let me and others do that. However, most were eager to help in some way. I think we embraced this collective awareness that offering a hand to another person, especially a young person, was a shared value among all of us. Sometimes, there were those who would get self-important on a variety of dogmatic and theological matters, but the vast majority was far more concerned with lifting each other up, reaching out to one another, and offering opportunities for people to find and keep a faith life. Therefore, what began as an organic process of building bridges between different groups in an effort to best serve students at the university, by the mid-sixties had grown into an active ecumenical ministry.

From everything that we were seeing at the time, there was a clear need to branch out, offer services, and meet spiritual needs of all students, Catholic or not. This was especially pertinent in the anticipation of the new four-year university, scheduled to open in 1969. At the same time, it was also clear that no one faith tradition alone could effec-

Rev. David Steffenson, Fr. Mauthe, and UWGB Chancellor Ed Weidner

tively serve all the young people at the university. Therefore, the discussion became how a collective campus ministry could meet the needs of all students and all faith traditions, however prevalent or however small. So, sometime around 1967, several of us came together to form the Committee for Campus Ministry to the University of Wisconsin - Green Bay, and worked for a very long time to craft a "Covenant," a statement of purpose that was meant to be more inclusive than any document prior to it. This was our guiding instrument, the art form which we massaged for a very long time, declawing it from any offensive or excluding language, defanging anything that may be biting to someone else, and yet not diluting the essence of our individual faiths. It embodied our primary objectives: helping students at the university find God, foster a spiritual life, and become the best they can be in their own faith tradition while learning to live in peace and respect with those different from them.

All of us are like a bunch of colorful strings, finding our way in life and striving to shine as brightly as we can. I may be a blue string, and you may be a red one. Each of us carries certain characteristics and beliefs that are uniquely ours, but as single strings, our individual capacity is quite limited. On the other hand, if we grab a bunch of the strings together, and twist them, we will create a twine, which now has a lot greater capacity. If we pull on a twine, it will not snap as an individual string might; it is strong, resilient, and powerful. Make no mistake: each string will remain authentic to its own characteristics; I will always be a blue string, and you will always be a red string. However, by intertwining and standing together, shoulder to shoulder, we now have a significantly expanded capacity to do just about anything— or, as was the case with us at the time, we had the capacity to best serve our ever-growing and ever-diversifying student population.

Each of us was keenly aware that there are buzz words in any religion which set people apart, creating deep divisions and seemingly insurmountable gaps, and thus becoming the markers by which people behave in their daily lives. Therefore, the task at hand was not to simply write up a mission statement, but to carefully navigate profoundly sensitive waters of history and belief, in order to reach a harbor of mutual understanding and agreeability that was both soothingly pleasing and authentically empowering to all.

Our work was also helped by the institutional changes and wise prelates. Vatican II produced historic and powerful ripples that were felt globally, as well as locally. In our community, Green Bay's Bishop A. J. Wycislo, who served as one

Engaging with the community after service

of Vatican II Fathers and chronicled his experiences during Council through frequent letters from Rome, visceraly understood the needs and realities of our time. Wycislo was an open-minded and deeply ecumenical man, and he put his considerable support behind our effort—giving us the credibility and the resources to proceed.

In an ordinary setting, this deed would have been almost impossible to accomplish. We were certainly not the first people ever to come together to attempt a similar objective of reconciliation and understanding. However, in our case, each of us was deeply committed to finding a way, regardless of how long it took or how difficult it was. We knew that, in many ways, our effort was an experiment, but we were committed to its success. We were that same small group of thoughtful, committed individuals, which Margaret Mead talks about, whose dedication to change the world was unwavering. I don't know that we changed the world at large, or even caused the smallest dent in its sprawling existence, but I do know that our endeavor made a difference in the lives of those whom we touched. It certainly changed how each of us, who were directly involved with the project, viewed our own human experience and how we lived from

FROM FIRST NEWMAN CENTER — The stained glass window entitled "Finding of the Christ Child in the Temple" seems an appropriate window for the Ecumenical Center chapel at the University of Wisconsin-Green Bay, says Father Richard Mauthe, director. The window, which was blessed in June, is from the first Newman Center in the United States, St. Paul's in Madison. It was first installed there in 1910 and is from Austria. Only six windows remain from the first center, said Father Mauthe. The window was a gift to the Ecumenical Center from Mr. and Mrs. James Gierczak, formerly of Green Bay and now of Rockford, Ill. (Photo by Mary Harrison)

Hard at work at the Ecumenical Center

then on. It was no longer "me, me, me," but about me *and everyone else*, in the broadest sense possible.

And so it began.

A priest earmarked for parish life was now leading the charge, given to him by his bishop, the needs of his flock, and a deeply-seated inner drive, to set up a ministry, which would bridge groups that for many years were separated by one dogma or another, by one political play or the other, and do it in a way that was empowering and engaging, never letting the discord, intentional or not, get in the way of the bigger purpose. Although I spent the next twenty-four years in this role, of building and transforming the ecumenical ministry at UWGB, I was not alone in this endeavor. Many people played an essential role in our work, in making our effort successful, and it is because of them that this enterprise—one of a kind in the United States at the time—was possible. It is also because of them, and those who came after, that this effort still endures.

First, everyone on the Newman Center Board of Directors supported this effort and put their resources behind it. Then, others joined in, including the Rev. Dr. Charles Bagby, my soul brother; John and Jerry Van Den Wymelenberg, local businessmen who transformed our finances through their shrewdness and business acumen; attorneys Tom Olejniczak and Bert Liebmann, both of whom I've known since they were very young; Jim Madigan, of course; as well as various religious leaders, including the Rev. Roger Bourland, Rabbi Isaac VanderWalde, Rev. Charles Freuden, Rev. William Spalding, Rev. Robert Smith, Rev. Jack Wolter, Rev. Dr. Dean Kilgust, and Rev. James Samter. Then there were Al Loomer, Ija Korner, Jon Lee, Lowell Bartell, John Rose, Joseph Neufeld, Fred Baer, Paul Davis, Dale Strong, James Ruben, Jerry Olson, John Decker, Marvin Houghton, Judy Hierseman, Sue Kaufman, Richard Whitt, Lee Cranston, Don Carstenson, Sandra Moore, Frank Jobelius, Bruce Ehr, Tim Mangless, Ronald Dhuey, David Brown, Harry Peterson, Don Makuen, Robert Rupp, Richard Whitt, Louis Weinstein, Mark Schwallie, Sid Glazer, Bob Mallon, Dick Solboe, Bud Gaston, Paul Mathews, Gordon Anderson, John Stevens, Peter Foster, Eldon Olson, Joel Eller, G. Marvin Lowry, Albert Harke, Paul Giesler, Gary Straughan, Bill Knuth, Aria Gaston, Alvin Harte—all of whom served on our Board of Directors and various committees in those early days. There was also the late Rev. Dr. David Steffenson, who was hired as our first full-time Protestant chaplain. Although Dave and I never really saw eye to eye, and bickered quite a bit, he made a difference in the lives of students who connected with him (one notable example is Chris Stix, a nationally regarded research analyst). Dave was a very intellectual, political man—a product of the 1960s and 1970s political climate—and very passionate about environmental causes. Today, there's a scholarship in his name at the Center, and I am glad for it.

All of these men and women, as well as those whom I have inadvertently and regretfully missed to include in this narrtive, were the pioneers who shared in the vision of interfaith dialogue as a pathway to peace and mutual understanding, and they all poured themselves into our work earnestly. The Center and its legacy are a beautifully tapestry, an enchanting mosaic of people whose contributions have given life and vibrancy to this enterprise. They each brought to the table their authentic selves, a deep sense of vulnerability, a discipline to follow the better angels of their nature, as well as all the tools in their toolbox. All that allowed us to accomplish what we set out to do. Today, the pieces of their souls, as well as those who came through our doors over the last fifty years, are inextricably intertwined with the unlikely story and the spirit of that place.

Newspapers often wrote about my role in starting the effort, but while I may have been able to point out the way, and have certainly enjoyed the attention, our ministry would have never flourished without these giants. They had the zeal and the persistence to persevere during some trying times. It's never an easy feat building something that has a lot of deep opposition—centuries of it! But they saw the big picture and were unequivocally committed to building something that never was—an interfaith center at the heart of a public university—but was bound to change the lives of many.

Building the Centers, first the Newman then the Ecumenical—and especially the Ecumenical Center—was hard. There were many egos to please, many naysayers, many financial challenges, and there were even things within each of our subconsciousness that would arise, wondering whether what we were doing made sense or was it even right. Pretending that inner doubts did not exist would be insincere, and one episode particularly stands out.

The first Sunday we turned Ecumenical, Rev. Roger Bourland, who was then the Senior Pastor at the First Methodist Church downtown—one of the most prestigious and visible churches in town—came in with his wife and children and sat down in the front row, next to the altar, and watched me as I celebrated mass. When the time for communion came, it suddenly struck me: what will I do if he comes up to receive it? Maybe he won't come up, I thought to myself. Except, in

The Rev. Richard Mauthe says Mass recently inside the new UWGB Ecumenical Center which will be dedicated Oct. 2.

the spirit of true ecumenism that Roger embodied, all four of them did get up and came for the communion. At that moment, there was no more ifs, or whens, or buts, there was just "do." Behold the lamb of Christ, and I put the host on his tongue. As they walked back to their seats, I realized that I had just given the communion to four Protestant people. Did I just feed heresy? What was I doing? I was sure, as full as the room was, there was going to be some antsy Catholic who would call Bishop Wycislo right away sneering, "Look what he did now!"

Ecumenism sunk in. It is one thing to talk about ecumenism, or interfaith dialogue, and even collaborate in big and small ways, as we often did—exchanging choirs between different churches, at the Catholic Cathedral downtown and the First Presbyterian Church alike—but it is entirely another thing to give a communion to a Protestant pastor. We had crossed the point of no return—and I liked it. I felt proud.

The next day, expecting that someone had called Bishop

A joyful exchange with an old friend

Wycislo before me, I called the bishop myself; I was not asking either his approval or his judgement. I just wanted to tell him what had happened from my point of view. His response was terrific: "You cannot be surprised at all that I would have done the exact same thing," he'd said. And, in retrospect, I wasn't. While some other bishop would have likely said, "Shame on you," and then went on to suspend me for five years, rationalizing that it was not only a Protestant lay person, but a Protestant Minister, a part of the Reformation, which was against the Holy Roman Catholic Church. It was the Church which bestowed the ordination upon me, and as she had given it to me, she could also take it away. But thankfully, Bishop Wycislo saw the big picture: he understood the Kingdom of God went beyond a particular church or a particular dogma, and he also recognized the importance of symbolic moves, like this one, in order to demonstrate how serious, how determined, and how deliberate we were in our commitment to ecumenism. It was no longer all talk, or the organic interactions that transpired out of a need to assist our students. Instead, we took the institutional guidance of Vatican II and the spiritual energy which permeated the hearts and minds of the people before

The Ecumenical Center (now Mauthe Center) building; the bells are in the background

us, and we pushed forward. Change had taken place, in real terms, and we began to build something that had never existed before. And we had done so in Green Bay, Wisconsin.

Now, it was a matter of sustaining the momentum. Unlike many other endeavors, which are often driven by a clear and rational plan of action, we had no blueprint to follow. To make things more complicated, a trailblazing cause deeply rooted in personal beliefs—and the emotional consequences of such beliefs—requires constant focus and conviction in order to survive. In a job of an attorney, you can have a bad day or lose a case, but in the work of an ecumenical ministry—at that time, especially—mistakes of spirit were not easily tolerated. We had to prove that this new way of being, that seemed to fly in the face of hundreds of years of historical and philosophical conditioning, was a better wayforward.

Giving the communion to a Protestant Minister during a Catholic mass was a wonderful move in the direction of solidarity and of sharing love in faith. At the same time, this does not change the fact that as humans we have our own issues to remedy. For a human being whose fundamental condition is raw and sensitive, and insecurities are a common occurrence, it requires real strength to remain devoted to these newly found principles of acceptance. Just like self-love, and the love which is bestowed upon us through God's grace, requires daily reminder and practice, so each of us involved in this cause needed to keep our inner world in check in order to best serve those around us. This was a tough balance. As human beings, creatures of biology and of spirit, we are predisposed to desire the approval of others, even seek it. So whenever we see something out of ordinary, disapproved by the society at large or within the historical context, or even by a single person, that little doubting voice emerges, questioning whether what we are seeing makes sense. Likewise, standing up to defend what intellectually makes sense (or disagreeing with what doesn't make sense) is even harder. Therefore, we are perpetually challenged to choose—daily—the higher path.

This inner wrestling isn't reserved only for those in pastoral roles who are building an ecumenical center or tending to a different kind of emotionally, spiritually, and intellectually strenuous labor. Quite to the country. This perpetual skepticism and doubting, often derived from our multitude of fears, is a constant companion to us all. We each are faced with confusions in our daily lives, be it in our professional, familial, or deeply personal lives. How we reconcile it depends on the clarity and the strength of our values. For example, in our own families, we may see members who live their lives contrary to what we have been taught to do, or what may seem to make sense to us, or what we consider "right" or "in adherence to God," and thus we may be quick to judge it. This is especially true if people live their lives in a way that has traditionally and publicly been viewed as taboo within faith circles. For example, a person has no faith tradition they follow, or they don't believe what we do, or they're divorced, or gay, or promiscuous, or blue, or green ...you name it. It is only natural that we would encounter things contrary to what we believe in and wrestle with our reaction to them, but the real question is what we do next.

A lot of people reject others because they do not fit the

mold. Instead of trying to understand their brothers and sisters, selflessly, and loving them unconditionally, they close themselves off, holding on to the limiting beliefs out of their own fear, often failing at the very basic exercise of inner analysis, introspection, and debate. Unfortunately, this fear of leaning in—engaging deeply and seriously—in order to understand that which makes us uncomfortable, is what ultimately leads us to a limiting life, half-lived life, and to a lack of self-awareness.

Thousands of years ago, Socrates opined that the unexamined life is not worth living. Most of us try to examine our human experience as best as we know how; however, examining life is not a one time affair. It has to be a part of our daily practice. Doing so allows us to digest new experiences and continuously clarify, modify, and strengthen our beliefs and values. In other words, examining life pushes us to grow. Indulging in the inner doubts and questions freely, dancing with the perpetual skepticism while remaining open to what we might find, is essential to examining our inner workings for the sake of a rich, loving life. Having the courage not to ignore (and consequently condemn), but to seek to understand is what lands us in the fields of clarity, companionship, peace, and love.

Catholics in particular seem to be very concerned about being right. I am not so sure that is what we ought to be focusing on. People are interested in a quest and we have been giving them answers. We should be bigger and broader than that. Until we enter the mystery, there are no profound "what ifs?" and "how comes?" and "where do I go from heres?" Until we can let go of the boundaries that have enveloped us, there will be no deep introspection, the discovery of God's grace in its fullest glory, or even true and unconditional love. It's virtually impossible to discover these without losing ourselves in them, without letting go in order to find. We can never arrive at a destination we desire without going the distance. It has to be our own deeply-felt journey, not a journey passed on to us by someone else's own experience. Someone's experience can be instructive, but it is our own that is transformative. A true Christian knows, there is no plan B, only free and full abandon.

I never wanted to be right, only to waltz with God in the game of love, passionately and freely, asking questions and finding answers that soothe my soul. It's this freedom of thought, of being, of introspection, and of loving that fills us with light and allows us to follow in His footsteps, in the pathway of love. If we judge others, it means we have not embraced the dance with God, and we are not free, for we are all God's children, without exception or exclusion. Using our "faith" to reject others for whatever reason is not faith at all, but a self-serving, protective dogma which separates us from God without hope for redemption.

"Whoever does not love does not know God, because God is love." (1 John 4:8)

Pope Francis, whom I adore, understands this deeply. What he teaches is not easily captured in words, but his deep sense of openness is apparent in his actions and his teaching. To him, and to me, and to all of us who were building the Ecumenical Center back then—and still continue to believe in its merits—what is most sacred is to let these children of God be. Let people be who they are. Let them live, play, and seek God, and find love in a way that makes sense to them. Let them rest in the Almighty. They are of God, just like you and I. If God is love, then so are we all.

It is for these very fundamental reasons that I could never get into a camp that stomps people out, and neither should you. When we follow the script to a T, without room for mystery or wonderment, and when we endeavor to impose rules we understand poorly upon those whom we deem less worthy, or more sinful than we are, we might end up feeling—in a single, fleeting moment—both righteous and right, But, by shunning others, we inadvertently shut ourselves from God's grace; we get stuck in the dark purgatory of conviction, where stale waters slowly drown our spirits and the lack of light suffocates our soul. This all is too high a price to pay only to be "right" over some commentary, which neither helps nor soothes those whom we're meant to love.

And so this very fundamental belief and utter truth, became my guiding light. Every time my human condition pushed me to question, to probe, to fear, to wonder whether my actions were good and holy, whether openness and the diversity of human experience and connection with God were the way forward, I decidedly let the doubts move in only so far as I could understand them fully; but then they dissipated unequivocally in the face of this very fundamental commitment that stood behind the Center, and my own life's work: we do not stomp people out no matter who they are. No ifs or buts. *God's love for all means all.*

To build and then run the Ecumenical Center, in addition to clarifying inner commitments, drafting guiding documents, setting up the Board of Directors, purchasing additional space where the new university was rising, understanding who our emerging students were, enhancing old programs and developing new ones, and hiring another minister and a secretary, we also had to have a business plan to make our effort sustainable. We used the same approach of investing through involvement that had served us well at the Newman Center. We used the religious preference cards to understand what percentage of students belonged to which faith traditions, and then we asked each denomination to contribute that same percentage of our annual operating budget. This allowed us to run a humble, but effective operation.

Not all denominations were consistent or always able to provide, but they did their best. With 64 percent of Catholic students, the Green Bay Diocese and the Fond du Lac Diocese, which covered the areas where a majority of the UWGB students came from, contributed most of the funds;

the others met the rest. The United Methodist Church, the Congregational Church, and the Grace Lutheran Church contributed significant percentages, too. Our Board of Directors and various local donors also contributed for various capital projects or special events.

The problem we encountered among some of the individual givers was that they wanted a plaque on the altar. I remember receiving a call one day from a local charitable lady who had offered to give us $1,000, which in those days was a lot of money, in exchange for a plaque on the altar. I told her that I was concerned that because of the drapes we had placed on the altar, her plaque would not be seen well; instead, I had a better idea: "How about we put your name on the toilet seat, so people would see it all the time?!" I am not sure she liked my irreverence very much, but she got the point: the altar was not for sale. It belongs to God and to His people, of all colors, shapes, and sizes. I did not want one person, or one denomination, to claim the altar; this would have estranged others. I wish she had asked for a room, or a hallway, or a program to be named after her. That, we could do, and I hope many people make such contributions to the Center in the days, weeks, and years ahead, so that our endeavor will continue to thrive.

As I reflect upon the decades in my religious ministry, I am awed by how much religious stuff has got to do with money. I am sure if Judas had been well-cared for financially, he wouldn't have been a traitor. Thirty pieces of silver? Who could do it for twenty-nine? When I contemplate the reality of this core Christian story of betrayal, I wonder if a lot of emissaries in Rome were given adequate salaries, could a lot of things within the Church change for the better? As with any administration, you need to have the money to hire people to do the work. And then, if you don't have enough people or they're not paid well, it comes down to where the document is placed in a large pile of paper to determine when something will be addressed. The more pages I need to turn, the more time I am using, and the more time I can charge. If all those people in lower positions for whom the system has to work to make it operate efficiently, if they were all paid a living wage, the Church and society-at-large could be far better off. Money holds a lot of things back. If you're conservative enough, there's money, but as soon as you ask for a liberating experience, the means to get even a little bit ahead, everybody becomes nobody.

Unfortunately, with our work at the Center, the setup we had designed in terms of contributions did not last as long as I had hoped. Some of the fourteen that had joined in the very beginning began to say quietly, but definitely, that they would have to pull out and that they would not match the percentage of their students because they simply could not afford to be both ecumenical and self-sustaining within their own operations. At first, most stuck around in terms of collaboration, but as time went on, some of the commitments wavered. The nature of these relationships changed, because when there is no financial commitment, the voluntary contribution becomes weaker. In life, there are two levels of priorities, individual and collective, and when there is not enough, the collective usually suffers. Luckily, we had hedged our bets with multiple players and in several ways in order to secure the Center's sustainability, so when several denominations struggled to pull their fair share, these other alternatives filled in the gaps.

For the next ten-plus years, we continued to operate out of our two locations: our primary spot became the two houses we had obtained on Nicolet Drive, adjacent to the university. One of the houses we used; the other we rented to the university. The former Newman Center building on Hartung Street, which was transferred over to the Ecumenical Center, was used for special events or when we had a large crowd—which we often did, almost weekly. However, after a decade filled with weekly events, masses, and worship services, diverse programs and colorful speakers, as well as countless hours spent in spiritual guidance and deeply moving conversations with thousands of students, we were in need of a new building. This was especially true as we struggled to meet the growing demand at our now permanent location at the Shorewood campus. It was also quite confusing to students to have two different locations.

By the grace of God, the opportunity presented itself in 1981 through the generosity of the late Arlene B. Walter and the trust that was set up from her estate in honor of her father, Byron L. Walter. I never knew Arlene, but our mutual friends described her as very kind, spirited, and engaging, but also quiet and reserved. Her father was a local businessmen who made his fortune as the president of the Green Bay Hardware Co. and was considered one of the foremost community leaders for many years, contributing his time and treasure to organizations such as the YMCA. Unlike Byron, however, Arlene was not well-known in the community, so her decision to commit her family's estate—the largest single gift in the city's history up until that point—for the benefit of spiritual, intellectual, and humane causes within our community took the city by storm. Twenty-nine organizations benefited from $4.5 million in gifts; we received $675,000 for the construction of the new building. We were beyond grateful to the Byron L. Walter Family Trust trustees, attorney Fred Will, and businessman Dick Blahnik. Dick remains a friend of the Center to this day.

Just like when we endeavored to build the first Newman building nearly twenty years before, there were several major moving pieces that needed to be arranged and negotiated in order for the new building to be erected. First, we needed the money, which was squared away through the Walter family's generosity. However, to receive the grant, we had to donate our old 338 Hartung Street building to what is now the Encompass Arlene B. Walter Child Care Center. Then, we had to complete the land swap with the university, the arrangement I had made with Chancellor Weidner about ten years prior. The parcel, located between the UWGB Sports Center parking lot and residence halls, now privately owned by the Center, was not an issue; the concern was squaring away the university easement to get to the future building. In order to make sure everything was done by the book, we made arrangements with the state to donate our land—what was remaining of it after we had parted with a big portion of it ten years earlier—and two houses adjacent to the university's main entrance in exchange for this easement. After facilitating all the logistics locally and at the state level, this was successfully resolved. Then, we had asked Heinz Brummel to design this building as well, and at long last we were able to pay him for his services. Soon enough, in 1981, the ground was broken, and the construction of the new state-of-the-art building began.

My personal debt of gratitude for this building also goes to the late Rev. Dr. Charles Bagby, pastor at the Union Congregational Church, who successfully led this fundraising effort. Charles was very sharp intellectually and spirituality, he was a man filled with faith. His wife Marian was equally impressive, and together they made a terrific couple. They served the Union Congregational Church for twenty-one years, and were deeply loved and revered to this day. In my personal experience, Charles and I understood each other intuitively, like brothers. We'd spend a lot of time together over at the Congregational Church. He had this little room, a confidential office, to the right of the library and separate from his official office, where we would get together, drink bourbon, and I'd pour my heart out to him. He understood me as very few people could, and would always engage through vulnerability, camaraderie, humor, and love. Bagby possessed a unique ability to connect, to touch you at your core, and to make you feel understood without any caveats. His leadership of our board of directors was extraordinary, too, and his friendship even more so. I think of him often, and miss him even more.

Two other people who were instrumental in building our financial footing during those days were two brothers, John and Jerry Van Den Wymelenberg, whose entrepreneurial zeal, business acumen, and financial prowess ushered

Pro-Vocations

Photo by Father John Blaha

Father Richard Mauthe, diocesan director of the Newman Apostolate and part-time cook at the Chambers Island Retreat House, models the latest fashion. Father Mauthe was cooking at the annual seminarian retreat the Holy Name Retreat House at the end of August.

Fr. Mauthe and John Van Den Wymelenberg

another development for our ecumenical endeavor: the Ecumenical Foundation. Leading our finance committee at the time of the Walter gift, John had the idea to use his considerable business insights and invest the money, using only a portion of it for the construction of the building and then financing the rest. The logic was, the interest on the income would produce more dollars than it would cost to borrow against it. We could then use the difference to furnish the building, and also put into a foundation that would then support the Center's activities for the years to come, especially during particularly dry seasons. The Board approved it, and this little maneuver allowed the Center to develop another source of income that still endures, albeit in a limited capacity.

I was particularly close with John Van (as most knew him) who was a selfless man in his relationships, but a shrewd businessman. He made so many things possible for so many people, myself included. He was generous with his time and resources, and definitely his keen insights on financial matters. I am not sure how far the Center would have come had it not been for him. His family, too, was quite wonderful, and we took many trips together (usually to Mexico). The Vans were a storied Green Bay family, with stakes in the hardware

Fr. Mauthe and Tom Olejniczak

store on Dausman Street, a bank on Walnut Street (that is now, I think, BMO Harris Bank), and also the Downtowner, a hotel on Washington Street, which was frequented by so many of us, from the town visitors to Vince Lombardi and his Green Bay Packers. Jerry's son Paul now runs the hotel.

Attorneys Tom Olejniczak and Bert Liebmann were also instrumental in building and then keeping the Foundation going. I've known Tom for over fifty years, ever since his dad Dominic Olejniczak helped us resolve the East River issue. Like me, Tom, his wife Dawn, and his brother Mark were adopted, and this fact bonded us even more. Tom has been wildly successful, much like his father, serving on virtually every major board in the area, including the Green Bay Packers. He has also kept a watchful eye on the Center and the Foundation, and has also taken care of me for decades. Today, Tom serves as my guardian. It's a funny thing for a man of my age to have a guardian, but it is also a moving, comforting, and deeply gratifying thing to know you can, in life, build relationships that span half a century and endure a lifetime. Like Tom and his wife Dawn, I also grew close to Bert Liebmann and his wife Diane. Bert's parents had a cottage on the bay, a couple of houses down from mine, and I remember getting to know Bert as a college kid back home during school breaks. He was always brilliant, thoughtful, and insightful, and our friendship has endured all these decades, too. I always love seeing him at the Center; memories of decades gone by fly before my eyes each time I see Bert.

It must have only been by the grace of God that I was surrounded by such wonderful people, most of whom were exceptionally accomplished in their own right, and by sharing with us their time, talent, and resources, they and so many others allowed the Center to continuously grow and improve. By this point, some additional names had emerged in our midst, on the Board and the committees, including Thomas Haevers, Rev. Llewellyn Thomas, Rev. David Brown, Mary Jane Golueke, Allan Hartley, Cynthia Johnson, Janis Kohlenberg, William Kuepper, William Laatsch, Rev. William Lawson, Gerald Olson, Rev. Ron Pascale, Daniel Udvig, and Sue Whittemore.

Of course, there were countless others who were impacted by our work and whose names were not recorded, although I pray that the impact we had on them has continued to live on in their daily lives.

Like any other organization, we had our ups and downs, but on balance, we were living out our mission fully and passionately in various ways. No matter what may have transpired in the ranks of the Board, the various denominations, or the staff at any given time—and occasionally there were some hairy issues—what remained constant was our commitment to taking care of our students, as well as the many community members, who found a home at the Ecumenical Center.

Every week, dozens and, more often than not, hundreds of people would come through our doors in the pursuit of something. Maybe they were looking for a place to call home, a place of refuge and contentment—a "safe zone" where they could be authentic and raw, expressing what was deepest within them yet feeling completely safe and secure in our presence and in the confines of our space. Or, maybe they were simply quenching the thirst for belonging, companionship, and friendship. Some, of course, were seeking a formal and a structured connection with God and their faith tradition, and perhaps a lecture or two on the topics in social justice, theology, and philosophy. Others simply came by for a cup of soup and a chat. Our conversations were deep, our interactions sincere, and our bond everlasting. The interpersonal relationships forged at the Center often flourished to marriages, many of which I blessed both during my time as the director and long after. It was always terribly exciting and deeply moving to witness two people, who had met under that very same roof because of one of our programs, profess the ultimate for each other: their undying love.

In those awesome moments, I often teared up realizing that we played a role, however small, in facilitating the divine providence of love in the lives of these young people. Their stories, too, were thus another set of ifs, their lives seemingly separate yet inextricably interwoven through the works of our ministry. It may have been a chance meeting at a dance or a vulnerable moment during a stressful exam period that opened doors to love for many of our students. And, by now, many of the children of my students have also gone through the Center, leaving their unique mark and adding to the footprint left behind by their parents and those who had gone before them.

Our commitment to care for people and to better their lives was always clear, from the very beginning, and it still remains the guiding principle behind all of the programming at the Center. It has been over fifty years since we set out to do this, to affect people—all people—in ways that would make their lives worthy of God having created them. And I'd like to think we have done this extraordinarily well, in small and big ways alike. Through serious events, even mournful episodes, to the soulful and humbling ones, and all the way to irreverent and fun activities, all God's children who found their way to the Center, I hope, also found a way to some sort of transformation.

Whatever their reasons were for coming, I hope they felt loved too. Even if they were there to protest against us for some reason, from the bottom of my heart and through every fiber of my being, I wanted every single creation which grasped for our door to feel welcomed and loved. I wanted them to know that there was someone who cared. And I hope that they have indeed felt cared for. I hope that you, who are reading this, have felt that either from me or another person at the Center or, more importantly, from the spirit that imbued our cause. I pray that in this very moment, you can pause, put this book down and recall that one moment or a single interaction with the Center, or with me, that did something for you that was positive and enriched your life. Maybe you embraced us as a home away from home, and we welcomed you into our fold; or perhaps we eased your suffering and made you feel better for one day, one hour, or one second; or maybe we fed you; or made you laugh through an irreverent comment or a joke; or even a simple "hello." If we have done any of these things, and I trust you have taken this moment to recall them, then I will know with certainty that my life's work has been worthwhile.

Like my kindergarten teacher, Ms. Grady, I too hoped that a simple interaction, a moment of care and of under-standing, would improve someone's well-being and teach them something new, about themselves or about life. I think we have succeeded at this, because many of my students have become lifelong friends. Of course, not everyone could become a friend or keep in touch over the decades that have gone by, and there are many of my students and people in the community whom I've lost touch with over the years, but I still pray they have taken away from the Center and from our interaction exactly what they needed. Life can be tough, and unfair, so I dreamed that our call would be one of service, friendship, and love.

WHEN THE BELLS TOLL

I **always viewed our ministry** as a doorway to God, opening wide to Heavens above, and calling people, all people, into God's gentle and loving fold. In order to conjure this image into reality, I also dreamed that we would install a set of bells at the Center, which would toll as if saying, "Come, come! Someone is here, someone is listening, someone cares." This dream came to fruition right after our new building was built, when the Green Bay Catholic Women's Club, once again, came to our aid with a financial gift to help us construct the towers and purchase the bells. I was elated! But, as with any other project I took on in the past, I encountered a problem. This time, it was a matter of finding a set of bells. Apparently, getting a set of bells weighing several hundred pounds is a difficult project. This isn't a matter of going to K-Mart and purchasing them, so it took a while until we could secure them. However, in the end, the wait was well worth it.

In my quest for the bells, I called my friend Heinz Brummel, the architect of the building, to see whether he could help us secure two of them. As it happened, shortly thereafter, Heinz was traveling to his native Germany to reunite with his brother Gunther, a photographer in Munster, and it was during this trip that he learned of a small but well-known bell casting foundry, Petit & Gehr, forty miles outside of Munster in the town of Gesher, Germany. Gunther and Heinz helped coordinate the ordering of the bells, designed in the likeness of those at the Munster Cathedral, and were the first ever to be exported to the United States by this factory.

Soon enough I found myself taking a group of students on a trip to Germany to watch the bells be cast. Students

Dana Kuehl, Alan Vanness, Matt Federspiel, Rosemary (Rosie) VenderKelen, and Lynn Posival as well as our staff member Kathy Matzke joined me on the trip. I knew this would be an adventure, but I did not know that tears of joy

Gunther and Heinz Brummel

would flow as the molten bronze transformed into a holy bell. One of the students, with tears in her eyes, came up to me and said, "You know Father, I hope I live a long time,

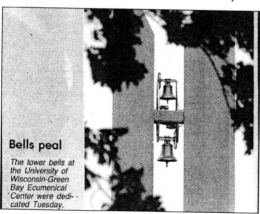

Bells peal

The tower bells at the University of Wisconsin-Green Bay Ecumenical Center were dedicated Tuesday.

From the Green Bay News-Chronicle

because I wanna be able to someday tell my grandchildren, I was there when these bells were cast." It was a marvelous experience that can hardly be summed up in words. Seeing this creation come to life was transformative. And the bells themselves, beautiful and enchanting, were inscribed by a simple line from the Book of Revelation: "Thanksgiving, Praise,

Special to the Press-Gazette

A craftsman works on a church bell at a small German plant in Munster. Two similar bells are being made at the Edelbrock firm for the Ecumenical Center at the University of Wisconsin-Green Bay. They are expected to arrive next month.

Blessing the bells: Bishop Wycislo and Fr. Mauthe

Strength and Wisdom to Our God, Forever and Ever," and they were hung, within two concrete towers, by the power of sheer enthusiasm and excitement of all those present. Keyed in a minor third, they pealed outside the Center for the first time on October 4, 1983; it was a Tuesday, and it was unforgettable.

The symbolism of a call coming through the slightly cracked doors, which the concrete towers represent, was unmistakable, as was the fate by which these bells arrived—spanning two continents, inspired by a dream of a priest, and achieved through a reunion of two brothers: Gunther and Heinz Brummel. Reunions carried a special meaning for the Brummel brothers, and this reunion was particularly fitting and meaningful. These two giants—standing like the bell towers holding our two bells outside the Center—broke the ocean to come together once again to hear the joyful sounds of the bells and of the excited crowds, much like on that day thirty-eight years earlier, in 1945, when as prisoners of war—Gunther at a British camp near Rhinebasse, Heinz at a British camp in Schleswig-Holstein—the two brothers were released and came home to their joyful mother. Not one son, but both of them, on the same day. The experience of that moment, of the bells rising and tolling loudly as a family was reunited once more, was unparalleled, and words can do little to convey it.

At the end of the classic 1946 film, *It's a Wonderful Life*, the little girl Zuzu utters the unforgettable line, "Every time a bell rings an angel gets his wings." Our bells have tolled for several decades now, including at Heinz's funeral in May 2016, when one of God's most beautiful and creative angels went home for another reunion with Gunther, his other brother Rudi, and their parents. After the funeral service at the Center, as we came to the cemetery, I watched four of Heinz's children honor their father, through an ancient tradition, by taking the dirt into their bare hands and covering his coffin; from dust to dust a giant went. And as his widow, Marianne, wept, I held onto her hand, and then placed a small token in it: an identical replica of the German bells cast from the leftover bronze on that fateful day in Gesher, thirty-three years before. The silence that followed, ushering gentle teardrops from our eyes, and a deep gaze into each other's souls, spoke volumes about the life we shared.

As we get older, and especially at my age, we see a great many friends go, leaving us with memories of beautiful days, and a heart filled with gratitude for the experiences we have had, good and bad alike, and a void, a hole in the heart, for the losses we have endured. I am rarely short on words, but for some things—like a moving opera, or a graceful waltz, or a peal of a church bell—there are no words to adequately describe them; like the loss of a dear friend, the emotions come down like an avalanche, rendering us unable to speak, and we can only feel, and thank God that we have had such a wonderful life.

THE NORMAN MILLER STORY

Whenever we talk about interfaith dialogue, I am reminded of an anecdote that illustrates the difficulty of engaging in the ecumenical business even when all involved are good people with best and sincere intents. It's a story of the late Norman Miller, a respected and highly successful businessman and community leader in Green Bay, whom I unintentionally offended over fifty-five years ago.

Namely, Norman was Jewish, and on one occasion, he and I were speaking at a gathering at SS. Peter and Paul Church in Green Bay about Judeo-Christian relations. In my attempt to be poetic and drive a point home of how we should all come together, I referred to Norman as my "estranged brother." To me, it was about the context in which, for many centuries, Christians persecuted the Jews instead of coming together; we were "separated," but still "brothers" nevertheless. To Norman, my calling him "estranged" seemed to build a wall, my words dismissing a tremendous amount of work he had done to bring about mutual understanding among various groups.

After all, Norman was instrumental in getting equal housing access for all races in Green Bay and devoted much of his illustrious life to issues of justice, so the last thing I ever wanted was to offend such a visionary and an ally. But those were the days of tension, and conflicts and misunderstandings were easy to come by, especially as we struggled to find the right words to express our deep emotion. However, Norman was a gentleman who never got in the way of my work; he exemplified the idea of rising above the fray. Regretfully, I did not learn about this offense until many decades later when it was too late to reconcile.

HOW I BECAME "PADRE"

One of the things that happened in the last fifty years is that the world has moved from formality to familiarity. People don't want to use terms such as Reverend or Father or Sister or Mother; this is Leona; she *is* my mother, but she's *still* Leona. This goes back to personalization and connectedness.

One day in the 1970s, Larry Boehm said to me, "Is there a name we can call you other than Father?" "Reverend, I guess, but that is even more awesome than Father, isn't it?" Out of that conversation, came the idea to "nickname" the Reverend Father (Me!), with a simple and endearing "Padre" or "Pa"—the Spanish version of the same thing. Larry almost single-handedly started calling me Pa, a tradition that continues to this day. In fact, there are people who know me only as Pa, and some of them call me every Father's Day, to wish me a good day.

In retrospect, I have come to appreciate the real value of switching these words around. "Pa" is a term of endearment, friendship, and familiarity with an inherent, built-in emotional connection that makes communication easier and free-flowing. Father, on the other hand, sounds like you're offering a deference, like you're in some court litigating a case, and it sounds serious and lacks vulnerability. As for my personal opinion on the issue, anything they want to call me is fine by me—as long as they call me!

Fundamentally, becoming "Pa" allowed me to better fulfill my priestly calling by making me more accessible to more people. It also inspired deeper insights about various aspects of our being, and the juggling of identities we all engage in. Who I am as a person feeds who I am as a priest, and vice versa. I've been granted access because I am a priest, but I have also been avoided for being a priest, too. We all embody identities that, on the one hand, open doors and, on the other, shut them. And, as much as we try (and as much as I have tried to get certain people to love me back) some simply won't. It is said age brings wisdom (good thing, because my good looks have left me!) and today I am much wiser and less concerned about those who don't love me, and more focused in making sure I appreciate those who do.

At times, our more formal identities, like being a priest, preclude others from being fully authentic and comfortable with us—not because they don't want to, but because they feel they ought to maintain some sort of decorum and deference. This creates distance. I have always tried to strike a balance between my various identities, inject humor, and be casual as a way of making others feel comfortable. That worked well for the most part. I will never forget one exciting party at a home of a dear friend where the regulars were joined by several new faces. Dressed casually and introduced to each other only by our first names, we were hanging out until late into the night. We were telling stories and laughing, and wine flew freely. At a couple of moments throughout the night, some of us got rowdier too, and our jokes naughtier. We had a great time! But by the end of the night, as some of the new faces—by now, new friends—were leaving, our host had asked them, "Come over, say goodbye to the Father."

One guy's face in particular was priceless! Shocked, he replied: "What Father, there's no Father here?!"

The host said, "Fr. Dick, would you come up and say goodbye, please?"

It was wild! And this type of scenario happened often.

Being a priest comes with a degree of trust. Some unhealthy people who entered priesthood have harmed this view, but by and large, priests are viewed as people of trust, and are given access and information that is very sensitive and deep, and it is our responsibility to handle such information with care. I have tried to do this always, regardless of how personal something was, or the closeness I had with that person. Trust is a very sacred thing, and must be protected even in times when it may cause us some hardship. For example, I've seen people make decisions I know they shouldn't for reasons I cannot reveal, because that would mean betraying someone else's trust. Seeing people make mistakes is hard, and knowing a way out, but being sworn to secrecy is even harder. But that is the price of trust and sacred confession.

Furthermore, we priests are also viewed with seriousness. I never liked this too much, because I like to have fun and think others should have fun, too. I also don't take myself too seriously. I will always cherish one particular time when I went to Los Angeles to visit my former student and his wife. I had married them, and after several years of marriage they had a set of twins; a boy and a girl. By the time of this visit the kids were probably three or four years old, and after seeing me around for several days, they got quite comfortable. One afternoon, the little guy came over to me, grabbed me by my hand, and said "bathroom!" His mom explained that he wanted me to take him to the bathroom. Easy enough, I thought, until she also instructed me to clap after he is done. All of a sudden, I am clapping over a toilet with two turds in there, thinking to myself, what the hell have I done with my life?!

Another funny story happened when a veterinarian prescribed a cream for my pet Schnauzer. There I went, all dressed up formally with a priestly collar, to a pharmacy to pick it up. And as he was handing the medication over to me, the pharmacist asked, "Are you going to put this on your hand?"

"No," I told him.

"Leg?"

"No," I said.

Finally, he'd asked, "Well, where are you going to put this cream on?"

"My schnauzer," I told him!

While we should *act* seriously when times demand that from us, we should not *take* ourselves too seriously. No priest or minister is better than anyone else just because they have a title, adorn a robe or wear a collar. We all put our pants in the morning, one leg at the time, and we all feel pain and love, and can be scared and lonely. (We all go to the bathroom, too.) To pretend it is anything other than that would be a lie.

There's also a public and a private part of us. There are things we might know about someone, because they told us; there are things we might project onto others; and, then, there's the whole area of possibility that nobody knows about. Each of us balances these two parts based on our comforts and values. Priests also have a private life that most people know nothing about—unless we told you. Service to the world and to the Church, has been my calling, but it did not come without a price to my personal life. The emptiness and loneliness of a celibate life has been a lifelong struggle for me. Likewise, being a priest in the ecumenical ministry, which I have loved, offered only one expression of a priest's job, and there are many others, too. At some point, to live authentically, we must wonder how else we might serve the world. We are all multitalented and multifaceted individuals; the question is not whether we have other interests and ideals, the question is whether we have the courage to pursue them.

My embracing of the term Pa allowed for a greater integration of the various pieces of me, and resulted in my greater ability to fuel my worldly works with my inner drive, and the fiercely burning love. It also allowed me to connect with the people who may have an issue with the Catholic Church, and me as a symbol of it, but they didn't have an issue with me as a person. Being Pa to thousands, Catholics and non-Catholics alike, allowed me to serve God's children in a way that went beyond the church walls, and into the hills and valleys of this beautiful Earth. It allowed me to help, and to serve, when and wherever called. It expanded my ministry beyond the ritual and collar into the pastoral work that needed to be done. As for me, life became richer because of it.

DANCE PARTNERS

Traversing through my life has been a wild, thrilling dance party and each person in it a different dance partner. I have had thousands of dance partners, and hopelessly wish that my dance card never fills up. Some of these dance partners stepped on my toes, and others danced so beautifully that I feel my heart swell with gratitude for the experiences, and a longing to repeat those moments. I am fortunate that a few of those especially compelling and skilled dancers danced with me for a long time, and some continue to do so. These partners came to me in different settings, but our waltz spilled over into all areas of our shared experience. Of course, my brother Ed is likely the longest (still living) dance partner I've had. At times, our age difference meant we didn't always dance to the same tune, but after many decades, we have formed a bond that few can rival. And, as we have both grown older, our music tastes become more aligned, and we now dance together perhaps more than ever before. Whether we engage in board games, reminiscing about our parents, or sharing insights and opinions on the world we live in, there's always some sort of a thread which strengthens and deepens our relationship.

Another lifelong dancer and one of my best friends has been Karen Kapp. I've known Karen since she was sixteen years old, and our lives have been intertwined ever since. We have vacationed together, held parties together, and even serendipitously found each other on the same flight after Karen's husband, John, died—all too young and all too soon—discovering comfort in our friendship, even when comfort seemed unattainable and the future vague. I remember going over to Karen's house that same year to decorate a Christmas tree; this attempt to cheer her and her children up turned into a tradition that still endures. Every December, we still come together to put up the holiday decorations and rejoice in the merry season. Karen has been

A lifetime of friendship: Karen Kapp and Fr. Mauthe

a stellar, fierce entrepreneur, and a true leader, a fantastic mother and grandmother, and a great friend. It was Karen also who took my beautiful yellow begonias after I moved out of my house on the bay.

The Norbertine Abbot Jerry Tremel and I've been friends even longer, and have shared many dances together. We used to spend quite a bit of time in those early days at Ss. Peter and Paul, and discuss the emerging issues of our time and the philosophical topics that educated, enlightened, and guided each one of us. Fr. Steven Brice has been a dear friend, too. He's a brilliant man, and a brilliant priest, too,

and will be the homilist at my funeral. I am beyond grateful that he agreed to do it—not many would dare—but I
know he will do a fine job. Another excellent priest and a
close friend is Fr. Tom Reynebeau. Fr. Tom is a pastor down
in Two Rivers, and I served as his assistant for a few years.
(Yes, I was assisting a guy twenty-five-plus years my junior—
what has my life come to?!) He knows me better than most,
including my deepest wounds and vulnerabilities. He's
always been an honest, straight shooter, and a man of great
depth. I am profoundly grateful for him and love him like a
brother. He's also got a wild sense of humor, too!

While in Two Rivers, I also met Karolyn Efferson
who was working at St. Peter's at the time and her husband Wayne who serves at the Nativity Parish in Green
Bay. Karolyn's now taking care of me, and is an extraordinary woman. I don't know how Wayne snatched her up, but
if he had not, I would have! She's a force to be reckoned
with, and her engaging and loving attitude keeps my aging
mind quite active.

Like the Effersons, or the Doerrs, or the Jauquets, or the
Hansens, or the Vans, or the Palubickis, or even the coauthor
of this book, I began my dance with different people at different points of my life. Knowing someone for a long time
does not necessarily equate being close to them; likewise,
some of the people I've met in my later years were God sent,
and have made a true difference in my life. Another duo that
immediately comes to mind is Mike and Sue Pankratz. Mike
is an excellent businessman and has been involved with the
center for the last few years. As for Sue, she has been the
best kind of a wife—she does not need sex and goes home
at the end of the day! Kidding aside, Sue has been my nurse,
my driver, and my friend since the early nineties. She's
taken care of me like only a truly loving (and patient!) friend
would, and I've been blessed for having her in my life.

Some of my special relationships were with groups,
like with the Knights of Columbus, the Green Bay Catholic

Fr. Mauthe and Sr. Ann Rehrauer

Women's Club, or with the Sisters of St. Francis of the Holy Cross over at Bay Settlement in Green Bay. I celebrated mass with the Sisters for many years, and became very close to several of them. My connection with them dates back to my childhood, however, since Sr. Paulette Hupfauf and I were peers, growing up together in Kimberly, and we both graduated from Kimberly High School. In the late eighties, when I became the chaplain of the Green Bay Serra Club, I'd join another Franciscan Sister, Mary Jo Kirt, and a few others in attending those meetings. One of this order's leaders, Sr. Ann Rehrauer and I grew very close, too, and I was blessed to have had a front seat watching all the good the Sisters have done for our community over the years.

The tapestry of my relationships has been incredibly colorful and enriching. To me, it never mattered whether I met someone at the Center, the student union, the grocery store, or at a conference in Philadelphia—they became my brothers and sisters. It is human nature to believe the world is revolving around us. This, of course, isn't exactly true. Our lives are tiny, but so unique, and we leave powerful traces on the world—and people—we touch, however briefly. Every interaction is an opportunity to impact another life, and every decision we make plants a seed, sending waves and ripples into eternity. This is sometimes called the butterfly effect, because a little butterfly flapping its wings in China, can cause hurricanes in Florida. The world is so intricate and interconnected, and I have lived my life aware that every look, every action, and every decision affects others in some way. Because of this, I always started with openness. In journeying through this book, I now can see clearly how this openness came about: it's a neat mix of my upbringing, my experiences, the reflection of a generation I was born into, and certainly the ongoing and everlasting conversations with myself and God.

Whatever it may have been, it placed me in a position

Sharing a hug with a former student: Ellen Mommaerts

where engaging with others came with ease and the desire to connect burned deeply within. Having the ability to connect with people from the outset, and not only in polite and chit-chatty kinds of ways, but deeply and genuinely, has been both an opportunity and a responsibility. It brings a smile to my face to think about all the various people who have come through my life, especially in those years of vibrant and wild activity at the Center and in the community. There were many, and I loved them all.

One lifetime friendship forged during these years was with a student, Luc Francillon, whom I met at a conference in Philadelphia. Luc came to Florida as a seventeen-year-old boy from Port-au-Prince, Haiti, where he joined his dad, and enrolled at a local community college. He had hoped to attend the University of Florida, but, thanks to the way those "ifs" in life materialize themselves, Luc missed the deadline. This is when a friend invited him to attend a Catholic conference in Philadelphia. Drawn in by the good content and social justice speakers, he signed up to come. But Luc never dreamed that this trip would ultimately lead him to Green Bay. And there they were, hoping to see the snow for the first time; they boarded the bus, and after eighteen hours arrived at their hotel in Philly. Four people were assigned to a room, and as life would have it, Luc was one of my roommates! You only have to imagine the expression on each of our faces when we realized that we were going to share a room. It was wild!

We spent four days talking about all kinds of topics, from politics to faith. By the end of the trip, I invited Luc to come with us to Green Bay, and he did. He hopped in the car with us—essentially, total strangers—and drove up to Green Bay, in January. I guess he was hoping to stay by the water at my cottage never realizing that in Green Bay, in January, you can actually walk on the water!

After multiple discussions, Luc decided to apply to UWGB that spring, and I made sure to introduce him to folks in admissions and financial aid. Luc became a stellar addition to UWGB, and was heavily involved in the Ecumenical Center and other campus activities. He completed a bachelor's degree in accounting in record time, and then went into the financial sector. He is now Vice President/CFO for Mars, and calls me often and visits me in Green Bay when he can. We talk about his work, his family, his beautiful wife and children, as well as current events and even philosophy, much like we did back at that conference in Philadelphia almost thirty years ago.

All relationships in life start off with a spark—we cannot

always put our finger on why or how, they just do. If we are open, they will happen just the way God intended them to. It is our job to embrace them, regardless of the shape they may take or their ultimate consequence. All relationships in our lives exist for a reason, some remain present for a season, and a few last a lifetime. The exchange that transpires through these relationships, however, extends into eternity. I have been blessed with many loving relationships, and have only ever asked, "How may I make it worthwhile? How can we dance together?"

Sometimes people miss opportunities to have relationships because they're too closed off, or they feel their position in life precludes them from doing so. For instance, one may say they're a teacher, why would they also be a

Like family: Fr. Mauthe with the Madigans and Bells

friend? As I've said previously, before all the titles, names, and accolades came about—and we neatly collected them as this short life zoomed before us—we were (and are!) a human being looking at another human being, while our souls have sought a way to go beyond the obvious, into the unknown, and reach that which is deepest within each one of us: love.

Why should we let the differences of our origins, age,

religion, or even our views preclude us from finding light within the other and sharing love with each other? We shouldn't. Had I done that, I would have probably been a lonely old man today. Instead, I am deeply loved, incredibly supported, and surrounded by the most wonderful circle, and my heart is filled with joy.

When I think of love, care, and joy, two other people immediately come to mind from my days at the Ecumenical Center. One is Ellen Mommaerts, an active, devout, hard-working student, who still calls me Pa, and visits often. Ellen is well-known in the community and is involved with the Norbertines as director of their volunteer community. Since both of us were adopted, we have always maintained a very unique bond and a deep understanding. I distinctly remember one afternoon conversation on the porch of my old cottage on the Bay, when Ellen and I faced the reality of adoption together, which can be difficult, even after so many years. Together, we were able to lighten the load a little.

Another person, always the life of the party, was Fred Bell. Fred married Cindy Madigan, the daughter of Jim,

Dr. Christopher Meyer and Fr. Mauthe

who was my first Newman Center supporter, and a lifelong friend. I have known Cindy since she was a child, and Fred's

personality and character only strengthened our connection and friendship. Fred was born in Canada, but lived in
Wisconsin for a long time, and he made a lot of deep and
meaningful relationships in both countries. He could talk
to anyone, engage with people from all walks of life in a
friendly, deeply compassionate, and caring way. He knew
how to work with people, and was a very open man, very
understanding, and very kind. When I think of him, I think:
Mr. Congeniality. Students loved him, faculty loved him, and
I loved him, too! He simply thought well of others, and also
about the world. He also had a very good business sense,
too, having built and run a highly successful computer business. It is often said that the good ones die young, and Fred
died in 2008 at the age of fifty-five. Taken way too early, but
never forgotten.

This was another example where one connection, one
path led to another wonderful one. I've been friends with
the Madigans for a long time, and we have shared a great
many adventures together—trips to Ireland and Scotland,
baptisms and celebrations—as well as times of grief and
loss, and the consolation that followed only because of our
friendship. These unbreakable bonds, in one way or another
and through the grace of God, have found a way to endure.
Cindy is now again involved with the Center the way she
was back in the day, first as a student and then a community
member. My friend, Jim, always remembers my birthday, too.
I chuckle at his last card along with a check—one dollar for
every year of my life!

Much like Luc, Drs. Christopher Meyer and Robert
Casteel were another set of friends whom I met during the
latter part of my ministry at UWGB. They were both excellent students, earmarked for the medical field, and now run
their own chiropractic practices in town. Chris, Robert, and
I spent a lot of nights discussing issues of faith and life,
laughing, drinking and cooking, and playing cribbage, too.
We had many conversations about the nature of Jesus, both
God and Man. I encouraged Chris to pursue the calling of

priesthood—and I did so for many years. I really thought he'd make a great priest, but I guess—in the end—he didn't think he had the calling for it. Instead, he dedicated his life ministering to the Body, leaving the care for the Spirit to others.

I taught Chris how to play cribbage, and one time (to help him play better) we decided to keep the score of wins and losses. I also felt he needed an incentive, so I suggested we play for a dinner—in Acapulco. As expected, he lost and was probably twenty-five or more games behind, so I conveniently took him to my favorite restaurant in Acapulco: steak and lobster at Coyuca 22. Having been to Mexico before, I think Chris expected to pay twenty bucks for dinner, so when he saw the bill in excess of $200, he was stunned. I had great fun with it, but he was determined to return the favor. Next year, when we returned to Acapulco, I had lost so many games of cribbage that I had to pay for dinner. I've pulled this bet many times on people, but Chris was the only one who had ever beat me so badly that I had to pay! Chris has been not only a close friend, like a son, but also my chiropractor. I do not do well with pain medicine, so adjustments that Chris gave me are probably one of the key reasons why I've lived to such an old age while staying mobile and active. I don't think it could have been possible otherwise.

Ah, there were so many people who touched my life in one way or another. Pat and Dan Udvig come to mind, Mike and Sue Watts, the Salms, Terry Martell, the entire Wright clan, and Tom and Kathy (John Van's daughter) Rolling. All of John's children were involved with the Center, and I have known them since they were very young. Ed and Mary Jane Selinsky come to mind, too. Ed was our music director for many years. Mike and Suzi Borlee have been lifelong friends, since the 1970s, when Mike first showed up at the Center with lots of questions, curiosity, and a deep zeal to learn. Mike's been a very successful businessma, too. I've also

Celebrating Fourth of July with Fr. Tom Reynebeau and other friends, and being goofy!

Playing cards: (l-r) Nate Smith, Joe VanDerven, Mauthe, Kyle Koeppler, Aaron Olejniczak.

One of the many vacation trips with friends.

been close with Rev. Bill Lawson and his wife Toni—they were my neighbors at the Bay, and as Bill is gentle, Toni is a spitfire. She'd never let me get away with some of my neighborly shenanigans!

As much as they have been rewarding, even essential to my life, relationships have also been difficult for me. Being an orphan created a yearning for love that was almost unquenchable, and yet, a calling into priesthood explicitly forbade any of the natural, biological desires for companionship and physical contact. I would be a liar if I said I did not wonder, from time to time, what my life would have been like with a human partner by my side. Perhaps the thirst for love would have been quenched and the loneliness eased up? Either way, a combination of these circumstances—one self-chosen, the other not—left me like a kid wandering in the fields of flowers, pursuing the enchantment of their smells, but never getting quite close enough to seize the fullness of their beauty. Greed is one of the seven cardinal sins, and I fear that I have sinned in my greed for love through relationships. After all, it was no coincidence that I took pride in those 800-plus Christmas cards I sent every year, or the four separate times I prayed for each of the 800: the time I placed the label on the envelope, when I placed the stamp on it, when I stuffed it, and when I sealed it. As I looked at each label, there well up a storehouse of memories about my relationship with each person. And yet, even as I gave my thanks to and for those 800, I always awaited something new: a newfound friend, an unexpected forgiveness, or a fresh insight. We all have things at various levels waiting to be born; for me, more often than not, I have hoped for yet another relationship to add to the tapestry of my life, another heart to open up to me and I to it, and another dance to enthrall me, rendering me speechless and my existence in God's earthly abode that much richer.

My dance card has been filled with so many wonderful people, and I wish I could include them all in this book. But there have been thousands, and I will ask for your forgiveness if I managed to not include you. Even the slightest idea that I might exclude someone pains me; it has been my life's commitment to never, ever exclude anyone. I don't think I was always successful at this, like I am probably not right now, but I have done my very best.

If it is some consolation, my co-author is going to have a hell of a time putting all these thoughts, names, and stories together! He wasn't even born by the time I began wrapping up my ministry at UWGB, but I made it clear that he must not forget anyone!

JOHN WAYNE AND I

I've lived a remarkable life, and relationships have stood at the center for it, but even as I met the likes of Pope John Paul II, I was never motivated by meeting celebrities. Meeting movie stars, musicians, politicians, poets was only great to the degree that they were thoughtful, insightful, or funny. Their celebrity status didn't mean

The Duke and the priest: Fr. Mauthe and John Wayne

much to me; their humanity did. However, there was one movie star who marked my generation: John Wayne. Those cowboy movies, while often completely unfair to the Native

Americans (and a little bit foolish), were cinematographic staples of my generation, and their protagonists were household names.

And so, during one trip to Acapulco, at a random stop at a local gift shop, I came across none other than John Wayne. I asked to take a picture with him. He was a giant of a man, both in stature and in spirit, and very gracious—and he agreed. Later on, as John chatted with others in our group, he found out I was a priest and yelled over to me: "Hey Fadder! You 'n' me got somethin' in common!" Considering his world fame and wealth, I wondered, what the hell might John Wayne and I have in common?

"If we want to do any serious drinking," John told me, "we gotta leave the country!"

He was right!

PASSAGE & INTERMEZZO

B y the early 1990s, inspired by the never-ending depth and enthusiasm of the students on campus and others in the community, I began to wonder what I wanted to do when I grew up. I was also slightly tired after thirty years of building, trailblazing, and functioning on four to six hours of sleep. Certain office politics at the time did not help either; my Protestant counterparts within the Center focused more on the political happenings of the period, the ebbs and flows of those changing times, and less so on the original spirit of our enterprise. Sometimes people in positions of authority would rather play righteousness and separate people than attempt to bring them together. As I witnessed more of this kind of approach happening within my own roof, I found myself feeling frustrated and tired, and was ultimately nudged to think of the next chapter. So, I began to wonder: If I died tomorrow, what would my regrets be? What would I want to put on my gravestone? The answer that came back was quite poignant and certainly in line with my past: *I wanted to be empty of all possibility.* That is to say, I wanted to exhaust the existence of who I am. I wanted to fulfill a lifetime—my lifetime. But what was that going to look like?

During this time, I realized that one of the things I'll go to the grave with is wondering what my son or daughter would have looked like; what kind of a person could I have helped them become? Regret is sometimes a very hard word, but I have at times regretfully wondered about this, and what my life might have been if I had chosen a different path. But despite those pauses, I would—could—never leave the priesthood and the work I was called by God to do. At the same time, I wondered if there was a middle-way.

Most of my life, I was pretty guarded, which came from my experience of being adopted. Although my adoptive parents were extraordinary, so was my sense of rejection and abandonment by a fifteen-year-old mother. I never really wanted to find my biological mother; I wanted to find myself and my place in this vast universe. Decades later, at an another intersection in life, I made the bold move of trying to adopt a child. Except, in those days, I couldn't. I was denied. I was a single man, in my early sixties: how was I going to raise a child? I was crushed. Why should I, as a single man and a priest, be precluded from having one of the unique joys of our human existence: having a child? Of course, you may argue—as did my friends and even myself at times—that I *am* a father to all those who need me, and not only one child. And, pragmatically, of course, the only way I could have fully and wholeheartedly embraced the challenges of parenthood, and given a child the love and attention it deserves, would have been by abandoning all else: the Center, the students, and all the others who looked to me as a father, either in a priestly sense, or simply as Pa. But abandoning it all simply in pursuit of my own desires would have ultimately been supremely selfish.

This experience of pursuing a child of my own reminded me of an important lesson about life and unconditional love I learned decades earlier: if we believe in our heart in something and want to pursue it, the path may not reveal itself as we had hoped, but that does not mean we should abandon it. Sometimes we get the short end of the stick, but things do even out eventually. The secret is in not giving up and understanding our own motivations. My desire for adopting a child stemmed greatly from my experience of having been adopted, and I knew that. So the ultimate drive was to help other orphans find homes. Not being able to adopt a child on my own did not mean I could not help others do that or help adoptive children find a place to call home.

About this same time, I decided that it was time for me to move on from the Ecumenical Center, leaving it with another generation, another group of people who would endeavor to take it into the bold, new century. The changes that followed the end of the Cold War, the fall of the Soviet Union, and the advent of the Internet, reminded me of the changes I watched in the 1960s. It was time, I thought back then, to serve at a quiet parish, where I could engage the congregation in a way they most needed. This was going to be a new challenge for me; it was also something that I had not done for thirty years. As much as I loved campus ministry, and all of my students—past, present, and even the future ones—it was time for the Ecumenical Center to be filled with new people, my office to be occupied by a new tenant, and a new vision to be put in place.

I submitted my resignation to the Board in 1991. They honored me by establishing a perpetual scholarship at UWGB in my name, and bid me adieu without much pomp and circumstance, per my own request. I often joke that I do a lot of outstanding things, but not neat things. However, this scholarship, and an opportunity to remain engaged and meet with the recipients, was neat. Also, I was convinced the Center would thrive without me.

I was appointed by the bishop to serve as an administrator at two parishes: St. Louis Parish in Dyckesville and St. Francis de Paul Parish in Marchant, just north of Green Bay on the way to Door County, and not far away from my home on the Bay. (Where, by the way, I began answering my phone as, "Hi, this is Dick at Dycksville, how can I help you?!") I loved it. People were wonderful, engaging, and faithful. I, on the other hand, loved the change of the pace from campus life to parish life, and stayed there until 1999 when I "officially" retired. But, since I am not exactly one to retire quickly, I kept serving as a weekend assistant at various parishes in Door County for another ten years, and for several years after that at the St. Peter the Fisherman Parish in Two Rivers.

Another project I took on as I departed the Ecumenical Center (and until very recently) was traveling across the country and abroad to raise funds for the Christian Foundation for Children and Aging. Today, they have a different name—Unbound—but maintain the same mission of helping children, young adults, and elderly find a home and the resources to live a meaningful and dignified life. I was particularly drawn by their efforts to raise funds for orphaned children, and have spent a great amount of time volunteering as a missionary for this cause. Since the early 1990s, I've been fortunate to help support more than 6,500 orphans in twenty-plus countries. I think my own experience and my passion for this cause made it difficult for people to say no to me, and because of it all, these children benefited. I am profoundly proud of the work we did and grateful to Unbound, their remarkable staff, and all those who selflessly and generously donated to support these children. Together, we did a marvelous job, God's work in its most fundamental and direct form, and impacted the lives of thousands. I am confident these children will do the very same thing and a lot more for others all over the world when their time comes. Such is the nature of service and partnership, and of a bold vision in service of God's grace to the most vulnerable among us. The emotional and spiritual benefits of this work are enormous, too.

Over nearly two decades after my departure from the Center, I had a lot of opportunities to contribute in different ways, reflect on my life and all that might come beyond this earthly realm, and also spend time traveling and learning. My earliest inclination to seek truth, wisdom, and to learn as much as I can never ceased. I always believed that we die the moment when we stop learning and contributing, not when our body gives up, so I continued fiercely and passionately to stay involved, keep my calendar full, and my mind active. Even today, as I am cooped up in this retirement home, I still look for ways to contribute, and be involved. What else is there if not to wake up, thank God for another day, and then give ourselves fully, freely, and selflessly. This attitude keeps life fun, our demeanor light, and our purpose of service still intact. It also, unmistakably, leads us to love.

RETURN HOME

Leaving the Ecumenical Center was not easy, especially for a "control-freak" like me. For a while, it was quite difficult, and I often felt as if a part of me had been ripped away. Indeed, the Ecumenical Center was my proverbial child, and the emptiness that followed our separation found me disillusioned at times, wondering where my life had gone, and asking God for a drop of grace to light the path before me.

I was also worried. As time went on, I watched the Center exit several decades of the renaissance and enter a period that seemed both strange and disconcerting. The directors who followed me were decent men and women, however, they lacked multidimensionality, which is necessary—even essential—in that job. The Ecumenical Center had been born out of a desire to come together regardless of our background or our beliefs, and recognize God in each other. This understanding sometimes seemed forgotten.

I believe that God created all of us exactly as He intended, and it is up to us not to question Him, but to love His creation, respect it, and embrace it. This enormous being who labors in each of our pasts, presents, and futures; the Father who gives us life and guides us through the journey of the soul, as we find a way out of brokenness into wholeness, and from imperfection to perfection reflected in the unity with and love for one another; the divine that imbues us with wisdom and compassion and awe before the beauty of His grace—cannot and does not possibly wish upon us divisions, hatred, and suffering. No, all three are exclusive products of our fearful human condition—a mindset that prevents us from seeing the big picture.

Claiming our own as better than someone else's while putting down another is nothing but a reflection of a fearful, lost soul wandering the pastures of His kingdom, without seeing the light and the love that abounds. In each of our days, there are many opportunities for us to recognize God's image in another or, on the contrary, to keep staring in our own image whilst fearing our own shadow. I have met many people over the course of my long life, and have concluded that we all need but a little bit of encouragement to come together and let go of the limiting notions of betterness in order to embrace togetherness. Our fear of those unlike us, and our refusal to engage them, stands in a stark contrast with our inner desire for love. We seek acceptance, but believe we can only be accepted by those like us. It is for this very reason that we gravitate to those whom we know. But that is easy, and limiting. Going after what we know, laying low in the comfort of our own perception, even limitation, is not what we are meant to do. Embracing the stranger, finding our divine self in him or her through friendship, is what leads us to making this world worthy of God having created it. Reading and quoting the scriptures, praying at the church or the synagogue or the mosque or the temple, asking and accepting the forgiveness for our sins, but then walking through our life by rejecting those who need us the most, is hypocritical and anti-God.

In the matters of faith, proverbially-speaking, we are sometimes like a bunch of dogs in the field, who hear another dog's bark in the distance and realize that out there somewhere is a fox. The first dog hears the second dog's bark; the third dog hears the second; the fourth hears the third, and you go down the line. By the time you get to the last dog, he doesn't know which sound he's chasing, but he is in the race. That's the way a lot of this goes: somebody has seen God, and they say, "woof," and there it goes, the pursuit of God ... until you come to the last dog, who doesn't know what he's chasing, but he is chasing. He heard the call. All of us are in this dog-like line-up; we are somewhere in there: we more or less hear the voice, or think we heard the voice, and need to go find it—or follow others.

Some of us go at it on our own while others join hands with like-minded souls, drawing conclusions which are neither confirmable nor deniable. The essential truth that often seems forgotten by many is that we are seeking the same thing; we have heard a call, and are pursuing it. How we get to it or who gets there first and who gets there second has little consequence on the journey. And I am not sure it matters to God, as long as we get there. The problem with some people is that they're more concerned about the process, claiming their process on the way to God to be better than the next guy's. Others claim they have already found God, so they need not search for Him; rather, they would teach us all how to find Him, too. Knowing how someone else has caught the proverbial fox is not the same as catching it ourselves. Having the opportunity to chase on our own, within the context of our own spiritual journey in this human form is a right we all ought to have. And I believed, and still do, that the Ecumenical Center was meant to offer this to people.

I love Pope Francis, because I believe he understands well the essence of the Holy Spirit, which works in and through each one of us. Rejecting this spirit, dejecting people because they're different than us, or preaching to them how they ought to be and live in order to be accepted is not Jesus-like; it is simply a product of our fragile ego. Unfortunately, so many I have seen would rather embrace fear than the courageous spirit of God.

This has also been true for many people since my departure from the Ecumenical Center. In part, the Directors lacked the ability and the stamina to paint a picture greater than individual desires, a vision that would pull people in, and keep them there for the sake of our community, our young people, and the world. Likewise, the denominations, struggling to keep their own doors open in the face of declining numbers of churchgoers, began to pull their support from the Center. And some people simply disagreed with the idea behind the Center. They could not fathom that a Catholic and a Lutheran and a Jew and a Muslim could share a meal together, talking about God from their individual perspectives, expressing what is most deep for them, and even engaging in a prayer without that threatening the other's beliefs. To these narrow, fearful souls, their God was somehow unreachable to all the others, and was better. Consequently, they advocated—some even quite fervently—against the Center, others thought turning the Center into a place for a weekly service is all that was needed, and some thought it was a good idea to turn the Center into a kindergarten! Finally, the nature of faith exploration also changed. Young people began seeking a different entry to God, which was one of those challenges I started to notice in the early 1990s. This last change wasn't bad, just different. The job of the Center was to recognize this, and evolve. Unfortunately, for a long while, it seemed that my child had lost its way in the face of changing circumstances and the lack of guidance that could help it see beyond the immediate pressures and into the future opportunities.

A great dancer knows that, as the song moves along, they too need to keep moving, to keep dancing. This is something I learned tap dancing as a kid, and later teaching others to do the same. The key to being a successful tap dancer is to, well, keep moving. Same is true for life: we must understand that life is never static, but it is always changing, always flowing like the river Rhine, and yet always staying strong and deliberate in its path forward. We cannot prevent change. The nature of change is, ironically, unchangeable. We cannot control it, we cannot resist it, we cannot alter it. We may try, but as we have seen from the annals of history, things will happen whether we like them or not. So, what do we do? Embrace it! We have to be quick on our feet. No matter how hard we try to hold on to the old, the new is going to come. The key is, then, to see beyond the narrative that we are accustomed to, and into the bold, multifaceted nature of the human and divine experience; to accept change like an old friend; to ask questions, for they may reveal new insights; and to stay open, because only then can the Holy Spirit work through us. When we are rigid, scared, and closed-off, there is no room for the divine to act within and through us. On the other hand, when we are open, we allow for those ifs of life to reveal themselves in a more meaningful and glorious way. Like that sign in the subway from a long time ago: let go and let God.

I followed this very same advice upon leaving the Center, and God shed the full measure of grace upon me, which lit up my path, and showed me new, different but equally exciting plan to work through me for the good of the world. New opportunities emerged and new relationships were born thanks to this new chapter. I embraced them with zeal, even as I struggled at times watching the Ecumenical Center decline.

Then, in 2009, the new leadership at the Center invited me to return. First, they sought to understand how the Center came about, what my vision was, and what I thought the future might look like. I was quite invigorated by this. The new leadership understood what the Center was meant to do, and then invited many others to join in. One way of doing this was through a "Tuesdays with Mauthe" program, which brought many old friends and current students at UWGB together on a monthly basis to talk about all kinds of exciting things. I felt things were finally heading in the right direction. And then, to my surprise and humbling delight, another thing happened: in 2010, they asked me whether I would agree for the Center to be named after me. This was a part of the broader initiative remember and honor the past, celebrate the present, and believe in the future—both the collective future and that of the Center. The Ecumenical Center was renamed The Richard Mauthe Center for Faith, Spirituality, and Social Justice, encapsulating three areas that have served as a hallmark of my life's journey, and have given me great joy and a great source of meaning, and hope-fully contributed to the world in a positive way, too.

I never thought that the small room at the UW-Extension Center where our Newman group first met back in 1960s would grow into a full-blown Ecumenical Center later that decade, and much less that this entity—now transformed and poised for a brand new chapter—would bear my name some day. I was truly moved by the gesture. In the newspa-per articles and official announcements, they referred to me as the "guiding spirit" behind the Center. Truly, it could have never happened if I had been a lone wolf in this endeavor. Quite the contrary: there have been many, many exceptional people who played a role in envisioning, forming, and build-ing this enterprise. Together, we showed the world what is possible when a group of thoughtful, caring individuals come together with a desire to find inclusivity.

I pray that our example will be an inspiration to those of you who are currently working to make a difference in this world, and also to those who are yet to come. God knows, this world needs more people willing to work with love and acceptance for the common good.

Well into the twenty-first century, the things that were taking place during our first efforts on behalf of ecumenism may seem quite unremarkable. We have grown accustomed to the pursuit of an interfaith dialogue. At a time when we see extremism rising all around us, both political and reli-gious extremism, it only seems obvious that we would seek ways to come together in the spirit of mutual respect. This, however, was not so obvious back in the 1960s. Today, there are many organizations which advocate for building such relationships among various, distinct groups, and I applaud them. I also chuckle when some well-meaning novice suggests that they're a pioneer in this endeavor. But I also keep quiet, because the quest for God, and for justice, and for equality, is much like a dog chasing his tail: it is cyclical.

The world has changed tremendously since those first days at Hartung Street. While the political discourse of the present time concerns me greatly—the language is vulgar, lies plentiful, and politicians' commitment to statesmanship and common good scarce—I am also hopeful that the progress we have made in many arenas, including respect for and appreciation of religious diversity, will continue to grow, benefit many more people, and endure regardless of the times that are before us. I pray that those whose lives were touched by me, the others involved in the Center, or by the Center itself, will continue to carry the beacon of light and inclusivity, the banner of peace and respect, and earnestly work for social justice for all God's creation. Yours, too, is a beam of light that travels through the dark night. At times, only the palest reflections of the moon will light your way, inviting fear and tremble in your midst; at others, the brightly burning glory of the sun will fall across your faces, illuminating the goodness you espouse as you offer warmth to those who most need it. Regardless, the path of God's justice and love must endure. I hope that you will be inspired and emboldened by the Center we have built, the spirit we have nurtured, and the lessons we gave to all those whose lives we have touched. We have set the course, but the work is far from over. It is up to you to continue it.

ADVICE FOR THE FUTURE LEADERS OF THE CENTER

Having witnessed a succession of inadequate leaders, I am compelled to offer a few thoughts of my own on the type of a leader the Center will need in the future. Just like the Center, which is highly unique, its leader also needs to exhibit a set of characteristics that would make him or her uniquely qualified for this role.

First, the person must be multidirectional, with the strong capacity to build relationships with people from all walks of life, and interact with highly diverse audiences. They have to be able to facilitate programs, offer guidance and consultation to students, while also engaging with community leaders, both lay and religious, for the purposes of fundraising and building alliances. It is important that future directors can focus on strategy as well as tactics, and on the Center's message. At the same time, he or she must administer the operation in a sound and disciplined manner.

I keep going back to fundraising, because many non-profit leaders can get shy when it comes to asking for help, especially in the faith-context, but director must be comfortable standing up before large crowds, or whispering in restaurant booths, deliberately asking for the needs of the Center to be met.

Second, they need to build relationships, and look at and appreciate differences that exist in our world, tempering their need to be right. If all someone wants to be is right, and not embrace the diversity of God's creation, then they cannot be the person for the Center. They must go out and meet people, get to know them, and allow them to know you—even as you disagree—because only then can there be trust. Support and commitment flow directly from this trust.

Third, the future Directors must be dreamers, they must be able to see beyond what is, and into what is possible, and be bold enough to pursue this vision even when it is hard. The vision, of course, must be inclusive, and the commitment unwavering.

Lastly, don't abandon because of the challenges, however small or big they are. God has placed those before you for a reason; you don't need to know the reason; you do, however, need to rise up to meet them … like the road from the ancient Irish blessing that shall rise to meet you in return as you fearlessly labor on this important endeavor.

I am an old man, near my last breath, but I hope that these insights can be useful to the future Boards of Directors as they seek to identify the Center's future leaders. I also hope that my friends, their children, and their children's children, will keep an eye on the Center, and offer their help whenever and however possible. Remember, life is a dance we all share in: it is never just me or just you, it is always *us*.

LIEBHABERTRAUM

One day, an eternity ago, I sat with an older priest who was in his nineties, and I said to him, "Fr. Bonnie, how do you know when you love God?"

"You don't know," he said, "but you always feel."

And I asked, "What does that mean?"

He replied, "God and I are like two lovers sitting on a park bench, watching the sunset, and feeling the presence of another; you don't have to talk, you just feel."

When we love, words can be inadequate and usually unnecessary. In those tender moments, when we feel deeply and authentically, our heart speaks of its own accord. It's long been said that the heart has its reasons which reason does not understand. Our job isn't to wonder about the reasons, but let the heart deliver the ultimate expression of God's grace: love. Once love is uttered, we have expressed the ultimate; no one needs to hear anything else but that they're loved. You love somebody or you don't. You don't say, I am practicing to love you! You just do. Either I do or I don't. And if I don't; you can't earn it, you can't buy it, you can't get it as a reward. And if I do, you just have to accept it.

It's the same story with God's unconditional love for us. We must accept it by feeling it; it will not come to full realization if we reason with it. And, paradoxically, we begin to recognize the depths of love and accept love by loving something or someone.

When we love, that love comes back to us in the most awesome ways. God showed me this most recently when the last baptism I performed—and perhaps the last I will ever perform—was of a child named Leona. You cannot but sit back in wonder at God's grace that has bestowed me with this unique gift, to baptize a child who bears by mother's name. How extraordinary! How incredible!

For many years, I chased God's love as an antidote to the void I felt, to the emptiness I encountered, and to the inadequacy I lived, not once realizing that what I was chasing had been with me, and within me, all along. Whereas, I was lost in my own search, blinded by desire and fear, failing to see that it was His grace that delivered me from sin to salvation, from fear to love. Every intersection in my life, every "if" seemed like a burden instead of an opportunity, every obstacle a reason to complain instead of grow. Such is the nature of life: when we fail to hear the sweetness of God's grace falling upon us, or His love, which is deliberate and unending, we get entangled in fears that prevent us from seeing that we are only a speck in the universe, placed on this earth to love and help our fellow creation on our way to God.

These fears drive us to reason and ration with the things that are not of this world, but of God; they move us to divide through the lens of religion, instead of to bring together through the power of faith. Afraid of our own shadows, we also curse those who love, because their love might be different than ours. In doing so, we forget that love offers no boundaries whatsoever, and it bounds across the mighty steppes of the universe without fear or favor. Love chooses us as much as we choose love; to reason with it is to replace love with fear. If you, even once, get in the way of someone's love, you have but prevented your own experience of it. Love will always find a way, and all of those who get in the way of inclusivity, of connectedness, of the colorfulness of life, will but walk away from God's vision for us.

As I inch toward my last breath, and step into the great beyond on the way home to my Creator, I am struck again by the constellation of ifs that have guided me like lampposts, from my emptiness into the fullness at the hands of your love. From one lamppost to another I traveled, and each dancer in my life's journey added a piece to the puzzle of my life, jolting me further away from the intellectual manifestation of love and into the visceral—the true kind. Each time I resisted my fear of relationships, or lashed out at those I loved the most, and who loved me back, I found myself falling into the abyss of the unknown and, consequently, needing your love ever more. And each time I felt love for my fellow creation, I was brought closer to feeling the awesome love of God. It was this love, unconditional and raw, that wove all the threads of my life into a beautiful tapestry, rendering me speechless at how abundantly loved I have been, and also somewhat inadequate at how little I have loved.

I'd hoped my life to be liebhabertraum, a lover's dream. When we fall in love with someone or something, we're always in love, and when we give of ourselves in service to love, we are no longer blind or afraid; we can see. The dream becomes real, and our love is reflected through our deeds. Love is not only a noun, but also a verb—love is all the actions we take every day to better the lot of others, heal the wounded, soothe those who are hurting, connect the divided, embrace the outcast and rejected. Love isn't only about us feeling good about ourselves, love is about making sure all the others know they too are loved. There's nothing more, or nothing less, we need but to be approved and unconditionally loved by another human being. It is through this love, through each other, that we see divine grace in action, and feel God's love for us.

After all, God appears to us through each other.

My dream has been that of a lover, wanting to make sure that all those who do not know they're loved can feel love. I realize that my own craving for this very same love is what inspired, what urged, and what drove me. But that was the only way any of this could have come about; had I not experienced my own pain of rejection, of loneliness, of sadness, of feeling unlovable, how would I have known of the burdens of others, or found a way to love you all?

We hurt, so that we can understand that life is meant to be so much more than our petty debates over dogma, politics, and trivial differences. We encounter many answers, so that we can engage with the mystery of God's grace of our own accord, and seek truth that soothes our own soul. None of us holds the exclusivity over God, because God is the truth, and the absolute truth is the love that connects us all.

Based on everything you have read in this book, you may think me a dreamer, and that is OK. You have to be a dreamer to pick up a book that says, *Once in Love, Always in Love* on its cover. We need more dreamers in this world, people who recognize that our ability to transcend the limitation of our earthly existence and connect to the divine within and without ourselves lies in our imagination. I have lived at the most amazing, extraordinary time in history, at a crossroads that could have blown the planet up or created some of the most spectacular inventions. And, while we haven't blown ourselves up—yet—we have come closer to each other. We didn't create the Internet out of a desire to be distant, to build walls, or to divide based on our gender, religion, neurological make up, skin color, nationality, political views, which God we pray to, or because of whom we love— but out of the fundamental human beat, an innate urge to connect, to belong, and to love. And so, I wanted this book to be found by someone out there, a creation wandering in

Fr. Mauthe received a princess tiara...   *...soon replaced by a king's crown.*
Fr. Mauthe with Wayne Efferson.

Dick and Ed Mauthe

There's a season for everything: for joyfulness, goofiness, and laughter;
for seriousness, remembrance, and profound understanding.
Every season, however, has one constant: togetherness.

the field of dreams, who can gain some insights from my own journey and the lessons I have collected over the years.

If you love, the love will return to you multifold. If you give, you will be given back. Live out your life and spiritual instinct boldly and courageously. Empty yourself of all possibility. No one is more blessed or more loved than you are. Never let those who attempt to put you down succeed, and never try to be something you're not only so you can fit a mold.

I've never fit a mold; I've been a misfit in many ways, and always pushed against the grain of those norms that intended to enslave me to fear, and preclude me from finding God's love. And as my last dance is nearing its end, I realize how truthful Fr. Bonnie was, how wonderful my lover's dream has been, how marvelous this romance with life is, and how much in love I have been all these years, and how abundantly loved I am.

Go on now, trailblaze a path that is worthy of God's creation and of God's love—no exceptions and no exclusions. Ever.

I love you.

AFTERWORD

Are you beautiful?" were the first words Fr. Mauthe ever uttered to me, yelling from down the hallway at the Mauthe Center, with a big smile on his face and an aura of light surrounding him. I will never forget this encounter, for two reasons: First, I weighed about fifty pounds more than I do today; I was this chubby kid, running around trying to be and become more. His question confused me. He, of course, wasn't talking about my physical appearance, but my inner beauty. He was inviting me to recognize that beauty within me—the very same thing he had done for thousands of others before me.

And, second, there arrived a lion: tall, charismatic, self-assured with piercing blue eyes, and the ability to make you feel like you're the only person in the room. It would take me years to fully understand where this confidence came from as well as recognize the brilliance in turning around his profound need for love—the need to be loved and accepted—into a driving force behind loving other people. Many of us, when feeling rejected, tend to lash out or, at the very least, drink the poison of bitterness ourselves, making us less joyful and more stern and critical. Not Mauthe. Even when he'd get upset (and I've seen what that looked like; it was not pretty), his commitment to transforming the anger and the hurt into joy and laughter, and love, was uniquely remarkable. That is what made him one of a kind.

As he lay dying in his hospital bed, surrounded by some of the people closest to him, only hours before he went to meet his Creator, I whispered to him that I loved him, and that he is loved by so many. He moved his eyebrows. He had told me many times that he knew he was abundantly loved, even as he never knew the love of a biological parent or a life partner. He sought this love elsewhere and, in the process, taught many of us what it means to choose love. It was his thirst for love that gave him the drive to pursue a better world. Sure, like all of us, he accumulated enemies who hated him for one reason or another, and that hurt him deeply. However, it never stopped him from following his bliss, from making meaning out of his spiritual journey, dancing his unique brand of a mystical dance with God, or from pushing himself to do better and be better in service to the Creator.

There were themes in Mauthe's life that shine more brightly than others, like the bright stars in an especially dark night. They include love, community, and impact; Mauthe's life was full of all three. In his last moments, he conjured an image of an extra large car, a vehicle by which all of us could travel together. His years of service to students and in the community rendered his impact uniquely lasting, even reaching the thousands of orphans in more than twenty countries who will never even meet him. And it's not only the people whom he directly impacted, but also all of those whom we have yet to impact because of all that Mauthe taught us. Lastly, it's love—the kind of love that is unconditional, yet very real. We are imperfect at love, of course, just as Mauthe was. But the issue of imperfection is not something that mattered to him much. What mattered is that we did our part, that we tried, that we fought to defy the ordinary, and that we loved the best we could.

I was extremely fortunate to have had the opportunity to

spend a lot of time with him, to gain insight into the wisdom he had accumulated, and have him share it in the last days of his life. It was in those last months, when he feared little except whether he loved enough, that I gained access to someone whose heart had been broken from birth, and for whom healing only came from all of those—all of you—who had given him so much. In turn, he had hoped to have given at least as much, if not more, in return.

Fr. Mauthe was a proud man; he was also courageous, deliberate, and authentic. He was unmistakably funny, yet so deep, and a "no b.s." kind of guy. He was a visionary who had the audacity to pursue something most resisted, and do it in his way. A lot of people talk about interfaith dialogue; Mauthe lived it. A lot of people talk about being vulnerable; Mauthe embodied it. A lot of people discuss God, religion, and dogma, but yet only a select few have the ability, the intellectual and spiritual prowess to get it, and yet continually search for more. I've met other people in their last days, but very few still engaged God in such a curious, fervent way that Mauthe did. A lot of people speak of authenticity, of service, of compassion; Mauthe demonstrated all these and more in ways that are both tangible and real. He made the spirit of Catholic social teaching—indeed, social justice in all faith traditions—come to life in ways that transcended the rhetoric, of which he was quite good, or the religious rites and sacraments.

Fr. Mauthe made all these come to life in the human form. For him, Jesus Christ, the son of God, could not be separated from Jesus of Nazareth, the son of Man. He brought God to thousands who sought a spiritual awakening by meeting them authentically. Mauthe knew that God does not come to us only while we pray in the pews of a Christian church, recite the Torah in a Jewish synagogue, meditate in a Buddhist or Hindu temple, or bow before Allah at a mosque. Divine grace appears to us every day, in every interaction we have with ourselves and those around us—but only when we let go of preconceived notions, judgements, and fear, and when we lean in to make sense of our human experience, our spiritual yearnings, and all that we do not understand. God appears when we push ourselves outside our comfort zones to recognize humanity and divinity in the people around us,

Fr. Mauthe and Adi Redzic

even as we, perhaps, wish to smack them.

Fr. Mauthe was not perfect. His egocentric streak drove some people away from him; his self-assuredness scared others; and some did not exactly get his "brand" of spirituality. But when all was said and done, what was left was a boy who spent his life searching for the love of a mother who rejected him, a romantic love he could never have, and an understanding of God who seemed fascinatingly mystical and awesome—and who did all this with a fervent desire and an urgency to better the lot of others, to offer that very same love he could not have, and to do so for the benefit of us all. Make no mistake, he knew how to take care of himself, too—just ask his cribbage opponents (he'd made sure they paid their dues!)—because he knew that only then he could take care of others. He was beautifully romantic, dreaming of a world that never was, and using the most primal and ancient instinct—a desire to belong—to deliver what we all crave: love.

Mauthe believed life is a wondrous romance, each encounter a new dance. Now, he's dancing with the angels. In life, he was a man with a mission: he wanted to love all God's creation. This mission translated into 31,975 days of hard work, faith, inspiration, and laughter. And a lot of fun, too.

Inspired by the mystery of life and of the divine, he sought to weave the lives of most disparate groups, embracing each of them with fervor and curiosity. He wanted to make this world a bit more caring, or, as he used to say, worthy of God having created it. And he succeeded. From the interfaith center he created, more than fifty years ago, the first of its kind in the United States with fourteen faith traditions under its roof, to helping find a home for more than 6,500 orphans, his impact sent ripples of love across generations, throughout the world, and into the universe touching the lives of thousands. In return, he, too, was abundantly loved.

In the hours before Mauthe died, a symbolic depiction of his life's work came into clear view: several of us from divergent backgrounds gathered around him to pray—all strangers in our own right, but friends because of him. Even in death, he brought us together.

~

Mauthe, you were one of a kind. You left the world better than you found it, you made us all think and feel deeper, and you inspired generations to think for themselves, to feel authentically, and to love unconditionally.

Goodbye, dear friend. It's been an honor to tell your stories and share your wisdom through the written word. We were so close to the finish line, and I'm sad we couldn't cross it together.

Have fun with that eternal dance...the party in heaven has just begun!

Fr. Mauthe:
In Their Words

One of the most important aspects of Fr. Mauthe's life were his relationships. He had thousands of them during his illustrious life, and he insisted that at least some of those voices be included in this book—*his final sermon*.

What follows, in an alphabetical order, is a collection of stories, memories, and insights shared by several of Mauthe's dance partners.

At the very end of this section is the text of the homily delivered during Fr. Mauthe's funeral.

By Fred Bell

(On occasion of Father Mauthe's anniversary to priesthood)

I was writing a letter to a friend of mine that I've been meaning to write for several years. I've thought about writing it during all those moments when you realize how precious someone has become—moments in your life when you're feeling on top of the world and he or she was there, moments when you're feeling bad and you see the concern on his or her face & you know that they'll be there then too. Sometimes that friend has challenged me, made me question my choices, made me rise above the limits I had set for myself. When I started to write, I realized that for this particular person, a great many people could write this letter. So, if you don't mind, I'll include you as co-authors.

When I sat down to start our letter, I discovered the perfect parallel. Most of us are familiar with the Christmas classic "It's a Wonderful Life," which stars Jimmy Stewart. His life is falling apart because the deposit for the Old Bailey Building & Loan Company was lost by Uncle Billy, and unless he comes up with $8,000, he'll go to jail. Well, in a moment of despair, he plans to take his life and plunge into the icy river. God intervenes, however, and sends Clarence the Angel (second class) to show him what the world would be like if he had not been born. Well, as the story is told, he comes to understand that he has played a vital role in his community, and it is, after all, a wonderful life.

By now, you may have realized that in this letter, Dick Mauthe plays the role of Jimmy Stewart. The parallels are very close. We sit here, in the Old Baily Building & Loan. The Ecumenical Center is a vital part of our lives that was kept alive and nurtured because Dick Mauthe knew it was important. At every critical moment of the Center's history, he turned away from other dreams and ambitions to keep it alive. When there was a run on the bank, he rallied supporters and challenged the community to rise up and preserve the Center and to realize how much we would be diminished by its loss.

In my own life, I think of the profound effect he has had. When my father died, up in Canada, far away from Dick and the [Ecumenical Center], my mind came back to Green Bay, to a Seder Supper. Ed Selinsky's choir was singing "Be Not Afraid," and Dick was teaching us about that rich tradition. To this day, that song and those moments bond me to my father. I think of how many times Dick has touched me and my family: baptizing our kids, sharing a meal, losing graciously at cards time after time. And I know he is a bit part of my life. Mostly, when I look out at this beautiful and dynamic place, I see my closest friends. I know that if you pull out just this one man, we would not be here... Our lives would have taken other paths, and some of us may never have met. But I wonder if we know how much it has cost him in his life to keep this dream alive. Just as Jimmy Stewart in the movie, is trapped by his commitment to his community and the Old Bailey Building & Loan, Dick Mauthe is bound by his commitment to his priesthood, and the Ecumenical Center. Now I know that Dick would argue that the blessings outweigh the price, and he's not about to jump in the river. But there are times, when he must sit alone, out past Dykesville, looking out at the frozen expanse of the Bay, and ask himself if it was all worth it. Well, when those quiet moments come, I'd like to ask him to just listen carefully to the quiet sounds and rustlings; because we are woven into them like threads in a tapestry, and we are grateful. So, in keeping with our tradition of sharing things to celebrate, I would like to celebrate Dick Mauthe: the Man, the Minister, and my Friend—with love and thanks.

By Mike Borlee

I first got to know Pa when my mother started to take my siblings and I to the Newman Center in the mid 1970s. As an early teen, it was easy to be embraced by his enthusiasm, and since I was working at a service station near the Newman Center, which was also next to his home, our relationship grew. I would see him regularly, whether it be for gas stops or car service.

In time, we became good friends and I would find myself helping him with various odd jobs that he needed done. In addition to his residence, he also had a cottage (aka the "tar paper shack") just north of Dykesville. Through the years, and various additions, the cottage expanded and became a transforming and transformative place for the mind, body, and soul of hundreds, if not thousands, of friends, relatives, lost souls, card players, and so on. During summer weekends, Pa would even hold youth retreats at the cottage; they were called Genesis Two. These were opportunities that helped you explore your faith, engage in serious conversations, and have fun...and always with great food.

I had the good fortune of being recruited to handle some of the mechanical jobs, mainly swapping out the lawnmower for the snowblower in the fall, and the other way around in the spring, and would often find myself hanging out with him and others at the cottage. It was a tough job but somebody had to do it! Those days and nights usually included great meals (Pa could have been a sous chef, or should I say a "soul" chef), a manhattan or two, and a good conversation.

Which brings me to one of the most interesting things about Pa. Conversations with him were not ordinary exchanges, but more like question sessions. He had this innate ability to converse by asking questions, and thereby make you look within yourself to seek and find answers. Many times, I would leave the cottage and, on the drive back to Green Bay, try to find answers. I know i was not alone in this. Everyone that spent time with Pa was engulfed in his warm embrace and enthusiasm for life.

At around that same time, Suzi entered my life and became my life partner. Pa married us, watched our family grow, and baptized our two children. We have both been blessed to be a part of Pa's extended world family. Because of Pa, the Newman Center--then the Ecumenical Center, and now Mauthe Center--became a regular stop, and an important link in our faith life.

I was blessed to be a small link in Pa's life chain; a part of the weekend sailing trips, the retreats, the transformation of the cottage, the dinners... Pa and I were in the Thursday breakfast club together, too. He would also host card playing nights at the cottage, and out would come the purple Crown Royal bag. We swore it was the loose change from the collection basket, but at the end of the night he was howling and taking all our money! Maybe it was a divine intervention?

There are many more stories and pieces of wisdom I could share, but I am going to leave you with this, as Pa so often did for me and others: My question to ask, why did God put me in his life?

Godspeed!

By Karolyn Efferson

My experience with Fr. Dick began about three years before his death. About a year after I met him, I received a call from Fr. Tom Reynebeau telling me that Fr. Dick's health was deteriorating and he needed some assistance with simple household tasks, shopping, etc. He asked if I would be willing to help. I willingly accepted as I had met Fr. Dick while he was helping at St. Peter's in Two Rivers and thought he had a great sense of humor. What harm was there in spending time with a funny priest?

My time with Fr. Dick seemed rather simple. The days were filled with picking up around the apartment, laundry, opening mail, reminding him to take his medications, getting him ready for outings, and fixing him breakfast and lunch, etc. As I witnessed his declining health, I couldn't help but notice the highlight of his days was welcoming guests in his home from all walks of life. He welcomed all of them with open arms and rejoiced in their arrivals. He was always thrilled to introduce them to me and tell me all the wonderful things about them. He had a way of making everyone seem larger than life! Ah, the pride and smiles upon their faces as he joyfully sang their praises. I'd quickly vacuum between the ringing of the doorbell and I'd find myself wondering, "What was it about this man that drew so many to him? Why were the young and old continuing to come and visit or take him out? What had he done that touched them so deeply? How could one person receive so many visitors, calls, and letters day after day?"

As I sat by his side and read aloud the letters he received from countless men and women, I began to see why this man was so incredible. Person after person expressed their gratitude to Fr. Dick for being with them through the many struggles and joys in their lives, for helping them on their faith journeys, for challenging them to reach for more in life, and for sharing in the sacramental moments in which God entered in, and mostly for being their friend. Upon reading these letters, I'd often look up to see tears in his eyes. We would sit in silence for a while and then he would humbly say how touched he was by what others had to say. He was so deeply grateful for each card and letter of thoughtfulness. It truly meant the world to him. I couldn't help but soak in those tender moments...those moments that illustrated the magnitude of his gratitude and love for his friends, family, and parishioners.

As the days went by, and his health and eyes deteriorated more, it became harder for him to get out and assist parishes with baptisms, weddings, funerals, and masses. This was hard on him as being able to do this was at the core of his identity. At times, we would sit at the dining room table and have mass together. As it became more and more difficult for him to see, I would read aloud the scriptures and we would talk about their meaning and how they fit our lives and the world today. He was always so deeply profound and insightful. I am forever grateful to him for giving me the opportunity to share in the breaking of the bread with him and giving me a greater glimpse into the magnificence of God.

I remember one day after he had moved into the nursing home, the nurse met me in the hallway. She said Father was having a difficult day and refused to get out of bed. It was late afternoon and I was concerned that something more serious was wrong. I entered his room to find him resting on his bed. I touched his arm and quietly asked if he was ok. He turned to me and said, "I'm fine. I just spent the day reliving my life. It's amazing how life plays out and all the beautiful people who enter into it." He told me over and over how grateful he was to have lived the life he did with so many wonderful people.

Fr. Dick was the kind of person who had a great love for life! He loved good food, good wine, and good company! This was a given! He knew how to enjoy the little things in life in a big way. He took great joy in being silly and enlivening everyone's' spirit. How could you not love this about him? I remember taking him for walks in the hallway at the nursing home and although he struggled to stay on his own two feet and often had to take sitting breaks, he always found something funny to say or do to make us laugh. If only we could all find joy in the challenges of life and share that joy with others.

My time with Fr. Dick was short-lived, but I was truly blessed to have known him. What I thought was going to be a simple task of helping a funny priest turned into so much more! Through his example, he taught me the importance of loving life and taking the time to enjoy the simple things. He reminded me often to cherish my family and loved ones and he taught me, above all else, to pursue the depth of love with every fiber of my being. I thank God our paths crossed and I will be forever grateful for the gift of his presence and friendship in my life.

By Wayne Efferson

I heard about Mauthe some thirty years before I actually met him in Two Rivers, Wisconsin. As the Director of Worship at Nativity of our Lord Catholic Church in Green Bay, Wisconsin, I often heard about the legacy of Fr. Mauthe and the work he did at the Ecumenical Center. In my role as Worship Director, I was often getting senior priests to assist us with the celebration of mass, funerals, anointings, and reconciliation. After meeting Fr. Dick, he agreed to help out at our parish. He was always most gracious to fill-in whenever our pastor was unable to celebrate a funeral mass with one of our parishioners. He mentored me in my first committal service at Allouez cemetery, and displayed his gentle and pastoral touch when a grieving widow needed consolation. I will always remember his compassionate approach with those who were grieving.

In addition to assisting us with parish funerals, he would fill in for weekend masses, anointings, and reconciliations. He was especially willing to assist with Wednesday mornings Mass with the St. Joseph school children. He committed to weekly celebrating the mass with the children for over three years until his health deteriorated. He loved interacting with the kids. Near the end, he would be wheeled up to the sanctuary in his wheelchair. At his last mass, all of the kids hugged or high-fived him at the rear of the church. He often told me, "these children were some of the best prepared children of the sacraments that I had encountered!"

From a professional standpoint, there aren't many priests like Mauthe. He was an excellent homilist, he was outstanding in his pastoral care, and he could lead like no tomorrow. Even in his final years, he was always willing

184 - In Their Words

to provide the sacramental moments for others and did it with excellence and compassion. He was an incredible priest and mentor.

Beyond the "professional" pastoral dimension I had with him, he was a true friend; someone I could confide in. What's amazing is despite his illness, he was able to lift anyone's spirit. I often told others, "if you needed a 'pick me up', go see Mauthe, he'll get you laughing." Mauthe loved to listen to the "Prairie Home Companion on Saturday evening radio. The stories were light hearted and funny, and I think he loved it because he was such a good storyteller too. This past Christmas, Karolyn and I got him the "Best of a Prairie Home Companion." He enjoyed those CDs in his final months and now that he's gone, I often listen to them in my car and I can hear him laughing at the "crazy" stories created by Garrison Keillor.

There are two significant priests whom I call friends, Fr. Jack Frerker, former SIU-C Newman Center Chaplain, and Fr. Dick Mauthe. Both had a profound impact on my life as a pastoral minister. They taught me to be a dedicated and faithful follower of Jesus. I still have a voicemail recording on my phone which Fr. Dick left on Father's Day 2016 in which he said, "...Happy Father's Day Wayne...I wish you a great Father's Day. Thank you for being a good one, thank you for being a loving one, thank you for being my friend...".

By Luc Francillon

I can unequivocally say that my life is truly richer for having met Father Mauthe in Philadelphia. It was fate that brought us together, to begin with, and the rest is nothing short of divine. I was attending the National Catholic Student conference in Philadelphia in January of 1988. In order to make the conference more affordable for over 500 students from all over the United States, four people shared a hotel room. My friend Marcio and I were paired with two people from Green Bay, Wisconsin: Father Richard Mauthe and Paul Mach, a student attending UWGB at the time. That chance encounter truly changed my life's trajectory, as I knew it. I intended to take a semester off, upon returning to Miami from Philadelphia. I had just graduated from Miami Dade Community College and had missed the spring semester admission deadline at Florida International University.

Father was fascinating and wise. I really appreciated his wit, sense of humor, and spirituality. We connected right away. I can remember chatting late into the night about all kinds of subjects ranging from Haitian politics to Liberation Theology. During the course of this four-day conference, through casual conversations, Father learned that I was going to take a semester off. He invited me to drive to Green Bay with him and a group of students from UWGB. I did not even own a winter coat, but I said yes.

We arrived at Father's house after 2 a.m. I was particularly excited to see the lake the following morning. To my bewilderment, the lake was entirely frozen and one could even walk on it! This was a truly foreign concept for a Haitian person, who had just experienced snow for the first time in Philadelphia. During my stay in Green Bay, Father mentioned that due to January interim session at UWGB, the spring semester would not be starting until February. He arranged a few meetings with folks from Admissions and the Business School, and I was really excited about the prospect of attending UWGB. I remember Father saying, "You just have to get accepted and get up here. Once you are here, I will try to help you any way I can." Thankfully, I was accepted to attend the spring semester.

Once I got to Green Bay, Father was instrumental in helping me secure several jobs on campus: Student Coordinator at the Ecumenical Center, Resident Assistant (how I paid for my room and board), Groundskeeping Crew, and Business Assistant for the Accounting Office for the University. I also benefited from a fantastic education and a degree in accounting that opened so many doors for me. Upon graduation, Father helped me get my first real job as an accountant for the Green Bay Food Company. I have worked really hard to create the life I live today, but none of it would have been possible without Father's unconditional love and his help.

What was truly transformational was the way Father took me into his life and introduced me to all of his friends. I learned about true Christian love and sacrifice. There were many other lessons and so many great memories with Father during my time in Green Bay: Learning how to build a raised garden, the joy of cooking, and how to properly do the dishes by hand conserving as much water as possible using Father's method. He was preaching "going green" before it was fashionable to do so! Not to mention the many nights spent playing seven-and-a-half (a modified version of 21). More importantly, Father taught me the value of one's word and unconditional love. All of these things have served me well both professionally and personally.

Over the years, we maintained our relationship through letters, phone calls, and occasional visits. There was never a dull moment with Father, always so charming and kept me laughing. Father flew to California to baptize my daughters Jasmine and Lauren. He married my wife Melissa and me in Two Rivers, Wisconsin in a private Mass that we will never forget.

Father Mauthe was one of the most influential figures in my life. He exuded love and I feel blessed to have been a part of his circle.

By Mary Hansen

Father Mauthe was an inspiration for so many and for so long, and if all who had been touched by his ministry had a chance to speak, the stories would be unending. I was fortunate to have known him since childhood. In reflecting on our relationship and how he influenced my life, I followed his lead in using the number "three" and organized my thoughts around three things: What I experienced; What I learned; and, what I view as a challenge. In fact, I shared these thoughts with him in a letter, on May 15, 2016, less than a year before his passing, and am including them here verbatim:

What I experienced "E"

What I learned "L"

What I see as a challenge "C"

1) Experience. In the beginning, there was your dog at our house. Actually, having a priest visit, walk in, call out, "HI, Ma!" and be part of the family was new ground.

Learned. Up until then, I saw the world as them and us. You made it a 'we' world in which it felt more like we had something in common with religious, rich, and city folks.

Challenge. Never let affluence, education, age, or experience influence acceptance of others.

2) Experience. On those lucky, lucky, lucky grade school days, we had you for our priest in the classroom for religious education. I still remember the first time I heard about agape love, empathy and God's reaction to each step in creation… "And God said, 'That's good'". I thought it was just your really, really cool handwriting on the chalk board that made you so special.

Learned. I came to realize it was the message. When Bert talked about Vatican II and how that changed his expectations, I realized that you were changing our expectations as we sat, and listened, and learned to live a different way. Since my eighth grade class left in 1966, it wasn't so much undoing what we had learned earlier, but more about doing what you and Vatican II proposed as a more Christ-like life.

Challenge. I have always felt spiritually at home in any church. I continue to read, explore spirituality, and pray that I do what God has equipped me to do in His service.

3) Experience. The Newman Center experience was very important. First at UW-SP and then UWGB with you and the members in the early 70's. Working with the liturgy group was my first experience in lay ministry.

Learned. It helped me understand the responsibility to be part of the planning and not just the recipient of someone else's work. Watching you 'preach' with several books open on the altar and an ever-present intellectual focus was certainly my first exposure to critical biblical scholarship. Didn't even know it had a name! And then there was the challenge to take the lesson and apply it to everyday life.

Challenge. And, that's where the lesson continues. How can I be better at living? Now I can add, "inclusive, love-based, and infection/take control" to the thought process.

4) Experience. Family dinners, weddings and funerals that include you have always been special times. You were with us through many of the major events in our lives to celebrate, counsel, and console.

Learned. It's easy to be in awe of your presence but I sense that you prefer to be engaged rather than fawned over. I feel like I might have missed opportunities to learn from you and share ideas with you. Good news...there's still time.

Challenge. Hold the belief that we are all God's children and respect the accomplishments and knowledge of others while still being accountable to bring something to the table.

5) Experience. The Family Living Class wedding at your place and 'reception' at Joe Rouer's was one of my favorite teaching experiences. We had done the 'weddings' in various churches with different pastors through the years.

Learned. I think what made the one with you different was the beautiful setting and message with open dialogue holding them to a more responsible standard.

Challenge. Continue to 'teach' by choosing the right setting and opening responsible dialogue no matter who the 'students.'

6) Experience. May 3, 2016 celebration.

Learned. Hearing the tributes to you exposed the depth to which your faith, family, fun, hard work, networking, intelligence, humility, risk taking, courage, resourcefulness, vision and love resulted in the accomplishments over the years. It's not the limelight that you sought but rather the valuable light that you provided for healing, inspiration, warmth, comfort and enlightenment.

Challenge. Take time to thank those who enrich life-both positively and negatively-for the lessons learned and the challenges presented. The question WWJD now with the addition, do my actions meet Mauthe Muster....inclusive, loving and infectious—taking control?

And so instead of a 'wee world' you have made us all part of a bigger, better 'we' world.

Thank you, dear good and faithful servant of God, for sharing your gifts with us. And thanks for the laughs along the way.

Rev. Bill Lawson

It was 50 years this past August, that my wife, Toni, and I arrived in Green Bay. I had been called as a pastor to Trinity Lutheran Church. Vatican II had recently come to a close, and the ecumenical movement was in its early stage. An ecumenical pastors conference had been assembled, composed of Roman Catholic priests, Protestant clergy, and a Jewish Rabbi. That's where I first met Mauthe.

At that time, if a Roman Catholic bride was going to marry a Protestant groom, the Protestant clergy could be invited to the Catholic church and participate in the ceremony, usually limited to maybe reading a scripture or offering a prayer. If the groom were from Trinity and Dick was officiating, he would call me to share in the service. Later when priests were allowed to come into a Protestant church for a wedding, if the groom was Catholic and the bride from Trinity, I would call Dick. We shared in many weddings over the years. One year in the spirit of ecumenism, I invited Dick to preach the sermon at Trinity on Reformation Sunday. It was a wonderful experience for the congregation and for him.

Later on, Toni and I explored the east shoreline of Green Bay looking for a cottage that might be for sale. We found one on Breezy Acres, the same road Dick lived on. When we told him of our find, he said, "That place leaves much to be desired. Get your earnest money back (which had been obtained from us illegally) and come and buy the place next to mine. We can have a lot of fun together!" At that point Dick became a prophet, because in all those years (and decades) living side by side, we sure did have a lot of fun.

First of all, I seldom had to visit a hardware store because of the inventory in Dick's garage, to which he gave me the entrance code. Later, he would tell people if he couldn't find something belonging to him, he'd go into Lawson's garage and there it would be.

One time, I told Dick that Toni and I were preparing for a trip to New Orleans. A few days later, he came over with a look of satisfaction on his face and said, "You will have a safe trip to New Orleans and back. I just blessed your car with Holy Water. I told him that was very neighborly of him, but the only problem was: we were taking our other car. He didn't know if the blessing was transferable!

There's also a remembrance involving sailing. One afternoon, Dick asked if I wanted to go sailing on the bay, on a good-sized boat belonging to his friend, Royal Shackelford. I agreed. As I was getting ready to leave, Dick came over with some kiwifruit that he had received as a Fruit of the Month gift. "Make a pie," he told my wife. "Do the same as if it were a peach pie. We will eat it when we get home from sailing, maybe around 10 p.m." It was 1 am by the time we got back, and as I walked into the house, Toni asked, "Where's Dick?" Being so late, I told her he had gone home. "Oh, no he didn't," she exclaimed! "Call him and instruct him to get over to our place to eat his Kiwi Pie!" And he did!

Another remembrance involves an anointing. On another sailing trip, as often happened on the bay, a storm suddenly appeared, developing high winds and waves. The bow of the boat was then turned into the wind. Amid the waves giving us a rock 'em sock 'em movement and the sail noisily flapping in the wind, we rode out the storm with no problem. Then we looked for Mauthe. He was nowhere in sight. Pretty sure he had not been washed overboard, he suddenly appeared from below the deck. He came up saying, "I thought we might capsize, so I anointed myself, but I couldn't find any water, so I used lemonade!" Like with blessing the wrong car, Dick wasn't sure whether lemonade was valid or not!

Friends would often tell me they heard about me from Dick's tale of two young Jehovah Witness women who knocked on his door one day. He told them he was a Catholic priest, but suggested they go next door, because the guy living there could really use some exposure to religion. You can imagine their confusion when they found out they were talking to a Lutheran minister--with Dick watching and smiling from his porch!

Apart from a lot of fun, Dick and I shared many deep, thoughtful conversations on a regular basis. Many Saturday mornings, I would go to his place for coffee and we would discuss weekly scripture lessons that both of us were using with our congregations, and share insights. When it came to sermons or letters, especially Dick's famous Christmas letters, he was extremely creative and a true wordsmith. You didn't doze off when Dick preached! Dick was also thoughtful and loyal. I remember one time, in later years, after some scheduling struggle, we had arranged a lunch when Dick called to ask whether it would be OK to reschedule; he had just learned of a death of a friend, and felt he needed to go to be with the grieving family.

I learned much from Dick, as a neighbor, a friend, and a pastor, for which I am grateful. The last visit with him was when Toni and I want to Odd Fellows where he was in rehab. As we walked in, he said to us, "I miss you and I love you". I regret a broken hip and adverse winter weather, which required Toni to represent us both at his funeral visitation. But, on his mass card of remembrance, he had the prayer of Saint Francis which ends, And it is in dying that we are born to eternal life. By our faith in the death and resurrection of our Lord Jesus Christ, Dick has inherited that life. May we all follow where he had led the way.

By Bert Liebmann

Sometime in the first half of the 1960s, I was told that I must meet a great young priest, then officially serving as an assistant pastor at St. Peter and Paul Church in Green Bay, but known to and among young people as that rare clergyman they could actually relate to. These young people spent time with him playing cards at a trailer he had at Chaudoir's Dock in Southern Door County. I did meet Fr. Dick Mauthe, but did not get to know him well until 1967 when I finished law school, married, and returned to Green Bay. By that time, I had absorbed four years of Jesuit education at Regis University in Denver, and three years at Harvard Law School in Cambridge, Massachusetts.

When I moved back to Green Bay (my hometown) in 1967, my wife, Diane, and I were looking for a priest and a community that understood the liturgical reforms and the broad implications of the Second Vatican Council. We found that priest in Fr. Mauthe. And that community was the UWGB Ecumenical Center. If Vatican II's theology stood for anything, it stood for the proposition that Christians of whatever background all needed to work together toward realization of God's Kingdom. And, not only Christians, but others of good will, also. So, Fr. Mauthe and others at the UWGB Ecumenical Center attacked the problem of how to develop that collaborative religious model in Green Bay, and were successful—developing a one-of-a-kind center in the United States.

Diane, my wife and my greatest asset, and I, thought of the Center as our parish even though we were formally members of other parishes in the early years of our marriage.

We, and our young children, were much involved with and identified pretty heavily with the Ecumenical Center. I also had the privilege to work with Fr. Mauthe for many years on the Ecumenical Center Board. Later we spent time with Fr. Mauthe at his cottage and vacationed with him in Acapulco, Mexico, but for him, at least, it was not pure vacation. Fr. Mauthe became a volunteer priest and a fundraiser for an orphanage organized and run by a priest in Acapulco. Fr. Mauthe also became involved in fundraising and explaining the work of some particularly worthy missionary projects bringing outreach to young people, and particularly to young people in need, in other parts of the world.

The Ecumenical Center community touched many students over many years. And, it brought a fair number of us from the community at large into weekly interaction with the students as Sunday liturgies were developed for both groups together. Fr. Mauthe's Mass was, of course, very well attended.

Pastoral assignment from the Green Bay Diocese took Fr. Mauthe from the Ecumenical Center and assigned him to the small rural church of St. Louis Congregation, in Dyckesville. Again, by good fortune, Diane and I and our children continued to have intimate contact with Fr. Mauthe, since we had a summer home, and more recently our principal residence, in that parish. Throughout his time at St. Louis and after his formal retirement, Fr. Mauthe always brought high energy, a vision, and a desire to help build the Kingdom of God and, to us, he became, in a very real sense, the face of God at work in Wisconsin. Well after his retirement, he continued to travel to Door County, to Two Rivers, and to other communities to assist with the growing shortage of priests needed to celebrate the Eucharist on weekends. Many times, he would preside at Mass as many as four and five times in a weekend, and deliver homilies at all of those liturgies.

A former UWGB Professor, who did not always agree with Fr. Mauthe, recently commented that Fr. Mauthe was a man of God who had really expended and exhausted all of his energies in his pastoral work. I agreed. In thinking back, I am reminded of Saint Paul who wrote about having "finished the race," having "fought the good fight", and having "kept the faith." Certainly, Fr. Dick Mauthe could have said the same thing. In current modern parlance, a radio or television broadcaster would say that Fr. Mauthe "left it all on the field." And for that, we can all be grateful. I certainly am.

By Jim Madigan

I met Fr. Mauthe in 1958 when, newly ordained, he was appointed associate pastor at SS. Peter & Paul parish. We became friends, and when the Bishop asked him to form a Newman Center on the UWGB campus, Father accepted. He formed a board and asked me to be on it. The Catholic Women's Club provided space for the new center. On our second board meeting, Father had the whole board on their knees... Well, Father offered to put floor tile in. Though none of us had ever laid tile before, he led, and we followed, and we did it. With him, we also had a lot of fun doing it.

Sunday Mass was a family Mass for faculty, students, & community. I can still visualize my granddaughter Maureen running at top speed down the hall at the Center, and Father on his knees catching her with a big bear hug.

The Center was soon ecumenical. The priests and ministers and rabbi of most of the faiths in Green Bay were happy to become part of what this young priest professed -- which is that God truly loves all of us. The Center grew to become a source of communication for students, students, & community. As the spiritual leader of so many, Father was always ready to move ahead, wherever God was leading him.

Never a hard word, but always a smile and willing to listen. Father Mauthe is truly a Man of God.

By Ed Mauthe

Growing up, Dick and I were always looking for adventure. One hot August day, Dick came up with the idea of biking to our neighbour's cottage on Lake Winnebago to go for a nice, cool swim. He asked, and I thought "Wow, what a great idea!" He asked Mom and Dad if it was OK, and they said "yes," knowing he'd watch out for his younger brother. So, Dick got on his Victory bike and I jumped on my used Schwin, and off we went. We were always challenging each other and so, of course, this ride turned into a race. Considering the 14 miles of riding and the heat of the day, that was a bad idea. But brothers will be brothers! So, we took off, Dick in the lead, and after a lot of pedaling, we reached Sherwood. Dick stopped to let me catch up and realized I was really wearing down. There was a bar that we went into, and Dick asked for some water for me. The bar lady called us both inside, took one look at me, and said I was having a sunstroke. Dick insisted that I rest, and I laid around, recovering, for a long time. I was still hoping for that swim, but he big brother said, "Nope, Ed. We have to go back home... slowly." And so we did.

Our parents, Ray and Leona Mauthe, dearly yearned for a child, and went through the adoption process in 1930. Finally, they received a word from the Green Bay orphanage, located behind St. Vincent Hospital, that their application was approved and that they could come choose their baby. Arriving at the agency, they were taken to a room with many babies. Our mother noticed one little blond toddler, sort of on the side, in the corner in the room. She said to the nurse, "We'd like that one." The nurse looked at them, surprised, and said, "Oh no, you want one of these babies," and pointed at the group of children at the center of the room.

"No, I want that child over there," our mother said. The joyful couple named their son, Richard Raymond Mauthe.

Since we were children, Dick was always very involved in debate competitions and extemporaneous speaking, and, unsurprisingly, he was very good. I'd listen to him and think myself, someday, when I am as old as him, I am going to speak like that. All my life, I would admire him as I listened to him preach with such elegance, deliver his positive message with strength and confidence, and tell a joke that brought down the house. I was 75-years-old when I realized that this baby brother was never going to speak like that.

Love ya, Dick!

By Dr. Christopher Meyer

I first met Fr Richard Mauthe when I was starting a new work study job during my third year at UWGB. I was the custodian at the Ecumenical Center as the Mauthe Center was then known. This was 1991. He was in his next to last year at the center and he seemed a bit intimidating as an individual at first, but as we interacted we clicked, and one day he invited me to come up to the camp. I believe this was in the Autumn of 1992. I thought it was to have dinner, as it was what he said, but it turned out that I was to be put to work first digging out a white birch tree stump that someone else had started, but hadn't finished. After that we sat down to dinner and the discussion that followed, began what would be one of the greatest friendships of my life.

I found in Fr. Dick a mind of outstanding complexity combined with a spiritual depth that I had never before encountered. I had seen much of the same traits in my own mother, and myself, so It was refreshing to find it in another person. We could discuss an amazing range of topics encompassing ideas and faith and everything else we could think to come up with. I have never before or since met anyone else like him. His compassion was balanced with real life experience and street smarts, his sincerity was combined with a mischievous quality that helped one keep from being too somber and serious as it is easy to do.

He was the first person who helped me see Jesus as both fully God and fully Man, and that he shared all the qualities and faced all the challenges that we do daily. (except for him being without sin) He was an avid collector of rich friendships, and I was introduced to a part of his entourage of diverse friends of many backgrounds, many of whom are friends of mine yet today. For that I am grateful. He helped me to develop my intellectual and spiritual and social/professional life.

I'm most grateful for his help when my father died of Cancer in 1996. His compassion and the time we talked really was a Godsend for me at that time. I had gone to school to be a Chiropractor to help alleviate suffering, but there was nothing that I could do for my own father. I remember reading a small booklet written by a priest who lost both of his parents in the same year. And in that booklet it described our parents as our first and most direct experience of God's love for us. And when a parent dies, that link is severed and it feels as if God has abandoned us.

Father Dick became in some ways almost like a second father to me. He was certainly my mentor, and he referred to me many times as his "Son". God must love me very much to have put Fr. Dick in my life in the way he did and the time he did. We became very close and enjoyed many evenings of dinner, drinks and discussion, as well as countless games of cribbage. We vacationed together for a week at a time in Acapulco 4-5 times, Florida once and Grand Cayman 4-5 times as well.

I was his driver when in later years he became reluctant to drive due to his eyesight failing, and we would travel for CFCA to churches from the Twin Cities of MN to Saint Ignace MI, and all throughout Wisconsin. We looked for the grave of Father Marquette by flashlight in St. Ignace with Father Pavel there after dinner one night. And we set off the burglar alarm in Oconomowoc, WI and had to wait for the police to arrive. We both greatly enjoyed our travels. We had many other stories too numerous to tell. We both agreed that it was good that we were not put on this earth at the same time, because if we both had been in our twenties and thirties at the same time, we would likely have both ended up in jail.

202 – In Their Words

How to encompass this amazing one of a kind man's life and our experience with him over decades is both an exercise in futility and extreme editing. He was like the Koch Snowflake: a triangle with smaller triangles placed on each side and so on ad infinitum. It is a figure with infinite surface area with a limited volume. He was a man of infinite complexity confined to a single lifetime.

I was truly honored to get to know him and have him as my mentor and "Second Father" He inspired me to be a better and more complete person and to embrace more and more of life. I have been forever changed and shaped by him and I will never forget him.

By Ellen S. Mommaerts

One of the most profound and deep conversations I had with Fr. Dick, while I was a student at UWGB and worked at the Ecumenical Center, was about adoption. We had shared lunch on his three-season porch at his home overlooking the Bay. The two of us shared our respective views and experiences of people growing up having been adopted. It was the one topic that I knew he could understand from the inside out and that his life experience might help me traverse the challenging path of understanding myself and identity.

Being of two different generations, the realities and logistics of adoption had changed a fair bit. However, the navigation of the emotional side of being adopted and the inevitable questions that come along with that reality seemed universal. He was curious as to why I would choose to search for my birthparents. He never had the desire to search for birth family members. WE talked about how the search might make our adoptive parents and family members feel and how neither of us wanted to hurt those closest to us in the world.

While we disagreed on this potential option of meeting biological family, I never felt judged by Fr. Dick, in the fact that I had searched, found and ultimately met some birth family members. He was able to walk with me in navigating my new reality of having questions answered such as:

"Who do I look like?"

"Why did they give me away?"

The desire behind the unanswered and always internal desire to be truly and deeply known and accepted was real. I was not looking for Fr. Dick to answer the questions for me but to listen, and hear deeply, the longings of my heart. I will be forever grateful for the conversation that day. Even as I recall the story I can hear Fr. Dick's voice reassuring me that no matter what choices humans have made on our behalf, God created me and loves me without condition.

By Thomas M. Olejniczak

"A Person with many names is loved," a proverb so aptly applied to Father Richard Raymond Mauthe, a/k/a "Pa," "Dickie Do," "Whisky Dick," "Uncle Dick" or "Brother Dick". There are a myriad of remembrances, accolades, thanksgivings and testimonies that can be written about Father Dick, but may I give you the perspective from someone who knew and cared for him for over 54 years?

I first met Father Dick as an 8th grader at St. Mary of the Angels School in Green Bay when he came to our family home to talk to my father about rezoning a parcel of property along the East River to allow for the construction of the Newman Center.

I had decided to attend a Franciscan Minor Seminary in Sturtevant, Wisconsin for high school and see what the possibilities might be for a religious vocation. During my four years of high school, Father Dick and I corresponded on a regular basis discussing my thoughts and aspirations and seeking his advice. The Priests censored our mail and I had many a conversation with our Disciplinarian about who this radical priest from Green Bay was. I guess "radical" in 1963 did not have the meaning it did in the later 60's, but all of his personal philosophy as reflected in this book give you a pretty clear idea of how Father Dick influenced my life.

I decided to attend St. Norbert College in De Pere after high school and our interpersonal relationship really blossomed during those years. My wife Dawn and I started dating at St. Norbert Orientation and we spent a great amount of time attending the programs and celebrating the Eucharist at the Newman Center. The fact that both Dawn and I were also adopted children really cemented our relationship with Father Dick. In fact, Father became an important part of our family from the start, officiating at our wedding, baptizing our children, burying our parents, vacationing in Mexico, and becoming our Chaplain at Fish Camp and Deer Camp for many years up until his passing.

Father Dick was intellectually brilliant, a voracious reader, a comedian, an uncommon challenger, a person who wanted to bring out the best in and for everyone. This book expertly captures Father Dick in his own words. It is easy to see why he received thousands of Christmas cards each year as he touched so many lives, all for the better.

I was blessed to be his caregiver and personal butler during his last three years of life on earth and although it was not pleasant to see such a vibrant, holy man slowly disintegrate; his wit and wisdom were with him until the end. There was nary a day that went by in which he did not continue his search for God's presence, for truth, and for an understanding of the workings of this world both with deep philosophical inquiry and comedic infusion. God made him out of clay, not perfect, but an original unrehearsed work of His hands.

By Sue Pankratz

I got to know Father Richard Mauthe on Tuesday, September 15, 1992. I knew "of" him, as he was my parish priest at St. Louis in Dyckesville. However, that specific night my world as I knew it changed. Where does one go but to your parish priest? We connected in chaos and discord; disconnecting in peace and quiet.

I could never call him "Father"; and when I did he would stop me and say "why did you call me that – you of all people don't do that?" "Pa" did not work for us and neither did "hey you." So I always used "Dick." When we were together, whether travelling or just everyday errands, we were often mistaken for father and daughter. During the course of our relationship, I was "his wheels," "his nurse"; he was my confidant, and the father I always wished for. I recall one occasion when I heard him tell some friends, "Sue is the best kind of wife—she doesn't need sex and she goes home at the end of the day." I was in the emergency room on more than one occasion with him and of course, the inevitable question, "And you are?" Dick would respond, "She and her husband are good friends of mine."

Dick was my annulment director. There is great truth in the saying about walking a mile in someone else's shoes. I thought this was simply another paper process one went through after a divorce to remarry in the church. I could not have been more wrong. One evening, when we were down at the camp and discussing specifically the issue of fairness, Dick brought out the gospel of Matthew 20:1–16, the Parable of the Orchard Owner wherein an orchard owner hires workers throughout the entire day, but at the end of the day pays them all the same. Aha! The light went on!

I still get teary when I remember the realization I experienced that evening. Dick had shown me, in black and white, exactly what I was really struggling with: life is not fair, and I got the crappy end of the stick this time. He also taught me that if you stay the course, life will reward you. And so it did. From that moment on, my life changed. While I would not forget, I could certainly forgive. And forgive I must, if I wanted to heal. I have Dick Mauthe to thank for that. What was certainly an epiphany for me, Dick told me later was also a deep moment for him as it came at a particular point in his career as well. While I never knew the specifics, I sensed that it was some of his "palace revolt" issues that were coming to a head.

During early 2000s, Dick said to me, "Where do you want to go for your big fiftieth birthday?" "Rome," I said. So, in late September, the three of us flew to Rome. Mike drove all of us to Venice, Padua, Florence, and Assisi. It was magical. I had reserved rooms at converted monasteries and convents; every morning Dick said mass in a gorgeous old and very small chapel. When we returned to Rome, the trip was highlighted by a personal (if you count 100 people) audience with Pope John Paul II. Retired Bishop A.J. Wiscylo, who was like a father to Dick, helped set the audience up. I had been told to take a dress, as "you never know where you will end up when you are with Dick Mauthe."

What I will miss most of all are the quiet and deep conversations with him. I once started a conversation with "Forgive me Father," he was quick to say, "You have never gone to confession to me in your life, and I don't want you to start now." The week before he died, Dick said to me "I am ready to go, Sue." My answer was, "You have to talk to the Big Guy about that." His was a quick to respond, "I have been telling him that, but he doesn't seem to be listening!" I consider having been given a great gift for I was alone with him when he passed on to his God—quiet and peaceful; just the way Dick had prayed for.

    This man touched countless lives, hearts and souls, and I am so very thankful and grateful mine was one of them. God had blessed us all with this marvelous man. Let us rejoice and be glad!

By Fr. Tom Reynebeau

When I think of Dick Mauthe, I think of his many passions, including...

Dick was an intense conversationalist. Total concentration was necessary, turn everything off that might be distracting. Look directly into each other's eyes and, by extension, each other's soul. The 20 questions would continue until all the present situation was uncovered and savored. Dick always had a desire to discover the deep connections that brought people together and gave life its meaning. If there was an image to be had that dug deep within the essence of life, Dick was all over it. It seemed that Dick had a mission to work within and through the lives of those he met so that the world around him could be transformed through many profound thoughts and understandings of life. This was his way of loving and caring for those around him, personally or professionally.

Dick had a strong desire to belong, to be respected and to be accepted. Dick sought to advocate for those who were powerless in the world; orphans and widows, ex-priests and religious, the hungry and uneducated, those unjustly accused, the mis-judged minorities and understood religious oppression within society as well as within the Church itself. Dick was very proud of his lifelong mission to uphold the 'underdog'. As an 'underdog' himself through his feeling of abandonment from his own adoption, he fought hard to make sure that everyone had someone who appreciated and accepted them. It didn't matter if someone lived near Green Bay, in Mexico, or anywhere in the world, if Dick could help in anyway, he did his best to do so. Likewise, Dick never was shy to advocate for himself. Many times, not long after a game, Dick would 'demand' the $1.25 he won at cards that night...there were no IOU's when Dick was owed something.

Dick was extremely loyal to those he loved. Friendship and relationships meant everything to Dick. Dick was a friend who was clearly focused on being just that...a friend. If you gained confidence with Dick, in whatever way, it was important to him that this relationship be clearly defined and carried out transparently. Dick had little patience for 'half-baked' friendships. Either you were a friend or not. With this in mind, Dick worked very hard to keep his many levels of friendship alive....from the 800+ names on his Christmas list to the few central figures that fed his soul...all knew how important they were to him. In personal relationships or societal organization, love had to be real with no empty promises or hypocritical dealings. True love improves the lives of ALL involved; ALL win or ALL lose.

Dick's faith in God was incarnational. This was the basis of Dick's strong intention to love. To love God had little meaning to Dick if it did not have 'flesh' attached to it. He had no time or interest in devotions or spiritual practices that didn't connect to the daily lives of the pray-er's life or the church community. To Dick, Jesus is Spirit and flesh, both human and divine. To fully live life, one has to develop both our souls and our bodies, and everything that falls between them. To make this happen, Dick's voracious appetite for education led him into deeper and deeper mysteries. Often Dick would end a conversation with the desire to think and pray further on the present topic. There was always more to examine and fit into place. When a challenging world event or personal challenge arose, Dick searched for the deeper understanding of the situation. With a willingness to dream bigger for a solution, he knew that there would always be room for hope and salvation. From his time at the Ecumenical Center to the many periodicals that fed him information and opinions, Dick's motto was that life was an opportunity to learn and not an excuse to hold on to our own prejudices and narrow minds.

Dick's love of music was a vehicle to engage life more fully. Emotionally, intellectually, physically, relationally, and spiritually, Dick moved into another realm of life that allowed him to transcend life as we know it. He would return to this world after his favorite symphony with a deep satisfaction and gratitude for the very molecules that eternally connected the universe that made that particular piece of music touch his heart as it did in that particular moment of time. There was no prayer deeper than the musical images that allowed Dick to touch the beauty of life and love present in that moment. I especially loved to watch and 'travel' with Dick as he reached an 'altered state' as he listened intently to his favorite music. It was a pleasure to experience these moments of ecstatic bliss with him.

Dick's life was Eucharistic. Dick fed countless persons. Dick's gatherings began with a desire to develop relationships, to define the intention for these relationships, to plan out a great menu with plenty of libations, to peel the potatoes and marinate the meat, to set up the massive table that held up to 20 people, to marvel at the amazing smells that emanated from the kitchen, to seat the people with great care as to who would benefit from the influence of the one sitting next to them, to a careful planning of the flow of conversation for the table itself, to present the food with great care and ascetic pleasure while music enhanced the mood, to Dick's prayer of thanksgiving and a raised glass that would delight the hearts of all present, to engage all the clinking noises of knives and forks working hard to feed the hungry stomachs of the guests, to the wit and fantastical stories spewing from the hosts heart and soul, and finally to the final mellow undertones of heavy physical bodies with content souls ready to continue on their personal journeys...this is the story of life, suffering, death, resurrection; Eucharistic joy and hope. What Fr. Dick prayed at the altar is the same prayer that brought people of faith together in Dick's heart and home. The Eucharistic banquet that spilled over into the everyday lives of the faithful.

Homily for the Funeral Mass of Fr. Richard Mauthe

By Fr. Steve Brice

SS. Peter & Paul Parish
Green Bay, Wisconsin
January 17, 2017

Greeting

Most Reverend David Ricken; brother and sister priests and religious; Ed, Joan and family; and all those who have come because you too love the Reverend Richard Mauthe: the time has come for us to say goodbye to this dear dear friend.

How can we possibly let this wonderful part of our lives go? Here's how we are going to do it. We are going to keep sharing our stories about him until our grief over what we have lost turns into gratitude for what we have been given. Then here at the altar, we will be able to hold him up, give God thanks for him, and place him back in God's all loving hands. That God might take him to his heart and into all the glory of heaven. And we might begin our next chapters in peace.

His Death

After decades of living on three hours of sleep a night and a "power nap" during the day, that body of his just wore out. He powered through it until December of 2014 when we almost lost him because of heart problems.

The winter of 2015 he became exhausted again and his body filled with infections. He went comatose. The doctors recommended he be put under Hospice Care. But he fought his way out of it.

This past Christmas Eve he presided at St. Peter the Fisherman in Two Rivers. He said he spoke about time, and the fullness of time. When time was full, the prophecies were all fulfilled, God came. Then Pa wept, before the full church. Perhaps sensing that his life had reached its fullness and God would be coming for him. The entire 800 people rose in standing ovation.

He celebrated two liturgies Christmas day, visited with Ed, Joan and their family. Every day the following week he was out visiting with people. Tom Olejniczak, his dearest of friends, companion and chauffeur said he just got exhausted.

A week ago Sunday he went to the Emergency room but was sent him home. Monday night he went back to the emergency room. This time they found a sepsis Pneumonia. The doctors said, they had nothing to fight it with. Pa said to Tom: I've had a great life. I have many of friends, I have influenced the lives of many people, I am ready to go. Sue and Karen's version of that was, his eyes were getting bad, he couldn't be in control anymore, he said "This isn't fun anymore, I want out of here!"

He began to go in and out of consciousness. The vigil began. Ed and the family stayed with him all Tuesday. That evening I guess they drew straws between Karen, Carolyn and Sue and Sue was elected to stay the night. About five thirty Thursday morning Sue was awakened by the activity of medical staff. She went to his bed just in time to be at Pa's side as he took a last few breaths...and died. He passed in peace.

He is gone. Pa is gone.

A Lion of A Man

We all knew him in so many different ways. Fr. Mauthe. Fr. Friend, as I learned last night at the vigil, Dick, Dicky-Do, Whisky-Dick and, like many here, I for years simply called him Pa. I say for many years because in these latter years, I began to see him differently. I began to see him as...A lion of a man. A lion of a man.

He was surrounded by his many accomplishments, like a lion's mane. Named one of the most influential people in the twentieth century. The first recipient of the Cardinal Newman award by the National Association of Campus Ministers. And as his dear friend Bishop Morneau pointed out, the only man in Green Bay to have two buildings named after him. The Fr. Richard Mauthe Center and...the Odd Fellows Home!

Certainly more important than these to him were all the children at the orphanage in Mexico he personally provided with clothing and food. How proud he was of the 6,800 children he found other people to care for through the Unbound program. And how he treasured the personal intimate relationships he had with countless people scattered throughout this country and beyond.

I think too of all of the talents and abilities that were so fully developed in him, like the muscled limbs of a lion. Like a front right leg he moved with powerful intellect, insight, vision, organization and leadership. Like a rear right leg he balanced the front with a servant spirit, empathy, compassion, readiness to sacrifice, patience in mending broken relationships and an endless capacity to care.

Equal to his intellect stood on the left his creativity and intuition as expressed in his love of liturgy, music, art, cooking, gardening and decorating. And balancing the whole body like a strong rear left leg was his spirit of play, of recreation and celebration, the joy he found in life and the affection he had for people.

Beating in this body was a royal heart. The heart of one who was no longer concerned with himself, but of one who had grown to be completely concerned with the well being of his people.

And through this pure heart and fully developed body coursed an energy so plentiful and so life giving it clearly came from beyond himself,. It came from all those who loved him.

Even after forty years I can still hear him roar across the Hartung Street Center worship space: "John Van? Everybody run. The ceiling's going to cave in! John Van in Church?!" We all laughed then too. That roar let us all know that life was good and we were in a safe and welcoming place.

Who here has not heard him roar as he slammed his fist down on the table holding the winning card in a cribbage match...Like a lion pouncing on his prey. Though as only his brother Ed could say: He wasn't really as good as he thought he was! I'm sure the pillars and rafters of heaven shook at the roar when that football went end over end for fifty one yards right through the goal posts with no time left on the clock in Sunday's amazing Packer victory. The roar in heaven must have been deafening!

But it was another roar of his that led me to first see him as a lion of a man. Back in 2012 the churches of the Wausau area were planning a series of speakers to mark the fiftieth anniversary of the opening of the Second Vatican Council. We had secured the great ecumenist, Bishop Sklba from Milwaukee to open the series. He would talk about the impact the council had on our relations with other Christian communities. Of course our Bishop Callahan would end the series to set the vision for the future. But we also wanted someone who could convey the spirit and experience of the Council itself.

I suggested to the committee that we bring in Fr. Dick Mauthe. They said: Who's he? Can he speak? I couldn't help but think back to 2007 when Pa preached at my twenty-fifth Ordination Anniversary Mass. We had agreed to use the occasion to renew the parish's vision of Church. Who could forget as Pa got more and more wound up with statements like: "In the Second Vatican Council the awareness finally broke in the Catholic Church that the Spirit is not the possession of the Church to be dispensed to those it deems worthy. The Spirit blows where it wills and it wills to blow everywhere! All life is sacred. All creation is sacred. The role of the church is to lift up that sacredness and to bring people into dialogue so that the fullness of God's Word might be heard." I'll never forget the grand finale: "The Second Vatican Council was the greatest act of communal mysticism the world has ever known."

Yeah, he can speak, I said to the committee. And! he has the personal journal that Bishop Wycislo kept while at the Council. Fr. Mauthe would be able to share with us his personal experiences while being there. The committee agreed to invite Fr. Mauthe who most graciously accepted.

Now the world had changed considerably between 2007 and 2012. The paralyzing polarization that grips our country had seeped into Wausau by 2012. As pastor I had been tip toeing around landmines afraid to offend one side or the other, worried about losing members and income.

The day came, and it should have been no surprise, but Pa did not follow the script. Instead of reading excerpts from Bishop Wycislo's journal, which would have no doubt been innocent and inspiring, Pa gave us his personal experience of the Council. "While Al (Bishop Wycislo) was over in Rome talking about ecumenism, we were doing it back here in Green Bay. We got 23 different religious bodies to all come together and sign a Covenant of mutual respect and cooperation. We created the first ecumenical campus ministry center of its kind in the country. When Al returned from Rome I showed him the Covenant ready for his signature. He was thrilled and so very proud." It would have been just fine if Pa stopped there. But then Pa veered off, pounding the pulpit for emphasis: "but now the Bishops are abandoning, if not betraying, the work of the Second Vatican Council!" He named names and made very specific accusations.

A fair number of people walked out as he spoke. I slumped down in my chair in dread as those who remained in the church gave him a standing ovation. After people had left he came up to me and said: "How'd you like that?" I said P...P...P...Pa! Did you see all those people who walked out while you were talking? "Yes I did" he said. "Good. That means they heard me."

As I looked at this 83 year old man, I realized it was a lion that stood before me. And the Church in Wausau had just heard him roar. When I came out of my reverie I realized that this lion was staring straight into my eyes. He was looking for something in my soul. It was then that I realized...he had not given that challenging talk for the sake of those who walked out, nor for those who gave him the standing ovation, but for those of us who have not yet found our voice.

But Pa, I wondered to myself. How does a man become a lion?

The Making of a Lion

No doubt fully aware his mentoring of this soul was not finished we sat down together this past October. He said he wanted to talk about his funeral plans, though now I believe it was about much more.

"I want to use the readings for the feast of Mary Magdelene for my funeral Mass." Quite surprised at his choice I asked him why. He handed them too me and I saw the first was from the Song of Songs, the mystical poem in which God is imaged as a Gazelle being hunted by the human soul. Then he recited to me the verses from memory:

> "I sought him whom my heart loves,
>   I sought him but I did not find him.
> I will rise then and go about the city
>   In the streets and crossings I will seek
> Him whom my heart loves.
>   I sought him but I did not find him.
> The watchmen came upon me,
>   As they made their rounds of the city;
>   Have you seen him whom my heart loves?
> I had hardly left them
>   When I found him whom my heart loves.
> I took hold of him
>   And would not let him go."

Referring to the Feast Day's Gospel he said: "Steve, like Mary Magdalene at the tomb, I have many times stood weeping, staring into the darkness of loss and rejection only to glimpse through the tears, love beckoning me on." He then began reminiscing about his life. It was a lesson in lion making.

At four years of age he stood weeping in the corner of the Franciscan Orphanage feeling lost and rejected. When through his tears he saw Raymond and Leona Mauthe beckoning to him. Come and live with us. That experience of rejection in those most formative of years forged in Pa a tremendous need to be acknowledged and loved. It could have been a tremendous problem all his life.

The wonderful Mauthe family poured love into this child's heart and brought forth that beaming-tap-dancing boy you see in the pictures here in church. Thanks to their love and support he succeeded in school and naturally went on to fall in love with a woman and become engage to be married. But as their relationship grew on, something more beckoned to Pa. He must have had a sense that the love his heart sought could not be provided be one, even very loving partner. He wept at the loss of her. But through his tears he followed this mysterious invitation. How fortunate that his heart was broken...open...to us.

After completing seminary and being ordained, this cocksure dynamic young priest went to Peshtigo for his first assignment. And was rejected by the pastor there. He was not even allowed to move into the rectory. Though no doubt painful, maybe it was a good thing to shake the confidence and humble the pride of this young priest. As he wept, the good people of SS. Peter and Paul Parish beckoned to him: come live and love with us.

There his broken and humbled heart was stretched open broad and wide. There he was mentored in the exercise of his considerable talents. There he was prepared for his thirty years of Campus Ministry.

We are all beneficiaries of the energy, fun, and rich spirituality Pa brought to our college years. He gave himself fully and deeply to us and to hundreds and hundreds of others: the liturgies, the retreats, the celebrations, the dinners, the parties.... then the weddings and baptisms; and in later years the building of the new Ecumenical Center in the middle of the campus. I remember when the bells from Europe arrived and were put in place. It was the crowning achievement of his life. He was as full of life and love as he knew himself capable of being.

Then it happened. Orders from on high to leave the Center and his Campus Ministry. Sorrow unto death! It crushed his heart to leave his greatest love. But as he stood weeping, peering into the darkness, he saw St. Louis Parish in Dyckesville beckoning to him: come live and love with us. Pa died to all things "mine" and rose more fully in the life Christ. God was fashioning in him a lion's heart.

Then he was told to retire and someone else was appointed to St. Louis, which he had given himself completely to and loved deeply. Again he stood weeping in the face of loss. This time the Door County parishes beckoned to him. When his advancing age prevented him from driving winter roads he left the many friends and new loved ones there. And St. Peter The Fisherman Parish beckoned to him, come and live and love with us.

Each baptism cleansed and scoured him. Each death and resurrection stretched his heart and deepened his capacity to love, until it was ready for the one it was made for. Until Christmas Eve, in the fullness of time, he was ready. He wept one last time, and began his departure from this world. And we know from the Song of Songs what happened last Thursday morning at 5:30 a.m.

"I sought him whom my heart loves,
I sought him but I did not find him.
I will rise then and go about the city
In the streets and crossings I will seek
Him whom my heart loves.
I sought him but I did not find him.
The watchmen came upon me,
As they made their rounds of the city;
Have you seen him whom my heart loves?
I had hardly left them

> *When I found him whom my heart loves.*
> *I took hold of him*
> *And would not let him go."*

Pa, thank you for never giving up the hunt. Thank you for keeping your heart open even in the midst of grief and loss. Thank you for speaking truth to power, for roaring! I pray you heard a bit of a roar today.

Amen

Amazing Grace

Amazing grace! How sweet the sound
That saved a wretch like me!
I once was lost, but now am found;
Was blind, but now I see.

'Twas grace that taught my heart to fear,
And grace my fears relieved;
How precious did that grace appear
The hour I first believed.

Through many dangers, toils and snares,
I have already come;
'Tis grace hath brought me safe thus far,
And grace will lead me home.

The Lord has promised good to me,
His Word my hope secures;
He will my Shield and Portion be,
As long as life endures.

Yea, when this flesh and heart shall fail,
And mortal life shall cease,
I shall possess, within the veil,
A life of joy and peace.

The earth shall soon dissolve like snow,
The sun forbear to shine;
But God, who called me here below,
Will be forever mine.

ACKNOWLEDGEMENTS

A depth of gratitude goes out to all who made Fr. Mauthe's story possible, and to Mauthe himself who was willing to tell it through a written word. I am deeply humbled for having been a part of his very last sermon, and pray that this book honors his legacy.

In addition to Mauthe, of course, writing this book would not have been possible without dozens of people who contributed in various ways to its creation and successful completion. I am especially grateful to Bp. Bob Morneau for writing the Foreword; to all the contributors, including the late Fred Bell, Mike Borlee, Fr. Steven Brice, Karolyn and Wayne Efferson, Luc Francillon, Mary Hansen, Rev. Bill Lawson, Bert Liebmann, the late Jim Madigan, Ed Mauthe, Chris Meyer, Ellen Mommaerts, Tom Olejniczak, Sue Pankratz, and Fr. Tom Reynebow; also, to Cindy Bell, Karen Kapp, and Peg DeSchepper for providing ideas, stories, and pictures, as well as to Hung Nguyen and the board, staff, and interns at the Richard Mauthe Center for Faith, Spirituality, and Social Justice for their assistance and support. Each of you have contributed in more than one way, and this book would not have been possible without you—your faith, feedback, encouragement, and patience have meant the world.

Additionally, I am thankful to Olivia Wendt and the Catholic Diocese of Green Bay for their assistance in fact-checking.

Finally, you would not be holding this book had it not been for Nevena Prebiracevic, who had encouraged this effort even when it was only an idea, and supported it ever since; Samantha Haas, who devoted her considerable skill to enthusiastically edit this thom; Kevin Strack, who helped with German translations, and my rock, Daniel Lestarjette, who helped with every step of this project, from designing the look of the book to spending countless hours editing and giving feedback, to overseeing the production.

I love you all.

ABOUT THE AUTHORS

Fr. Richard Mauthe (1929-2017) was a Catholic priest who spent his life fighting for the underdog, building bridges, and serving those in need. He is credited with establishing the Ecumenical Center (now Mauthe Center) at the University of Wisconsin-Green Bay, and helping find a home for more than 6,500 orphans in over twenty countries. In life, he was recognized by the first John Cardinal Newman Award for Campus Ministry and was selected as one of the Top 100 Most Influential People of the Twentieth Century in Wisconsin. Dick Mauthe was a lion of a man, who spoke truth to power to defend those most vulnerable in our society. This book is his last sermon.

Adi Redzic is a writer, entrepreneur, business and life strategist, and a professional speaker whose experiences during the civil wars in the former Yugoslavia imbued him with a zeal to help others, through word and example. His friendship with Fr. Mauthe culminated in this book, which is meant to educate, inspire, and enthrall.

All proceeds from the sales of this book benefit the Richard Mauthe Center for Faith, Spirituality, and Social Justice, a 501(c)(3) nonprofit organization.